FOREIGN MAPS AND LANDSCAPES

FOREIGN MAPS AND LANDSCAPES

by

MARGARET WOOD B.Sc.

Formerly Headmistress Newquay Grammar School for Girls

With 12 Pages of Maps in Colour
14 Illustrations in Half-tone
and Maps and Diagrams in the Text

GEORGE G. HARRAP & CO. LTD
London · Toronto · Wellington · Sydney

First published in Great Britain 1968
by GEORGE G. HARRAP & CO. LTD
182 High Holborn, London, W.C.1

SBN 245 59116 8

*Composed in Monotype Baskerville type and printed by
Morrison & Gibb Ltd., London and Edinburgh
Made in Great Britain*

CONTENTS

ILLUSTRATIONS

MAPS IN COLOUR

PLATES IN HALF-TONE

ACKNOWLEDGMENTS

The twelve map-extracts and Fig. 1 are reproduced with the sanction of the Government Survey Departments of the six countries concerned, and I should like to express my appreciation of their courtesy and helpfulness. I gratefully acknowledge the help received from Dr Beck, of the Landesvermessungsamt Baden-Württemberg, Dr Spicher, of the Swiss Geological Commission, Dr H. S. Verduin-Muller, of the Geographical Institute of the Utrecht State University, the Port Authorities of Amsterdam, Velsen, and IJmuiden, the Royal Netherlands Blast Furnaces and Steelworks (Hoogovens), the Norsk Aluminium Company, and the Royal Netherlands and Royal Norwegian Embassies.

I also thank the following for permission to reproduce or otherwise use photographs, maps, or diagrams:

Dr H. Furrer and the Swiss Geological Commission (Fig. 3); Messrs Oliver and Boyd (Fig. 5); The Director of the Survey Office, Baden-Württemberg (Fig. 6); The Director of the Mannheim Tourist Office (Fig. 8 and Plate VIII); The Managing Director, Port Management of Amsterdam (Figs. 9 and 10); Aerofilms, Ltd (Plates I and IVa); The Swiss National Tourist Office (Plate II); The Director of the Kandersteg Tourist Office (Plate III); Paul Popper, Ltd (Plates IVb, VI, and XII); Margaret E. Wood (Plate V); Robert Holder, Urach (Plate VII); The Norsk Aluminium Company (Plate IX); K.L.M. Aerocarto (Plate X); The Chief, Eastern Laboratory, Aerial Photography Division, U.S. Department of Agriculture (Plate XI); and my brother, Harold B. Wood, for preparing Figs. 2, 4, 6, 7, and 8 for the press.

INTRODUCTION

This book is an introduction to the study of foreign maps, and of the twelve map-extracts which are reproduced, ten are chosen from the official maps of five countries of continental Europe and two from the official maps of the U.S.A.

The maps selected are mainly of scale 1/50 000 or 1/100 000, and were in each case the latest edition available in 1966. The regions which they cover are all of great geographical interest, either on account of their clearly marked physical characteristics or because man has imposed upon the natural landscape a significant industrial or urban pattern.

It is obvious that these map-extracts represent very limited areas, and it is most important that the full map-sheet should be at hand, whether the whole sheet or only the extract is studied in detail. Moreover, the various tints used, the rock-drawings, hill-shadings, symbols, etc., must be seen in the original to be fully appreciated.

Six of the twelve studies are almost wholly confined to the reproduced extracts, but in the remainder the main features of the complete map-sheet are discussed. In the latter the extract area may be dealt with under a separate heading, or heavy type may be used for those of its feature- or place-names mentioned in the text.

Most studies are followed by a list of additional maps. Some of these are chosen to show the wider geographical setting of particular districts, others are chosen to emphasize more strongly some special feature. A selection of books for further reading is also included at the end of the book.

It should be borne in mind that no map is likely to be completely up to date. Even the time lapse between the land survey and map publication may result in changes in the countryside, and often a number of years elapses between the original publication and any extensive revision.

In many maps the symbols are very small and finely drawn, and a good hand magnifying glass is most helpful.

All maps may be obtained from Edward Stanford Ltd, 12–14 Long Acre, London, W.C.2.

Målstokk, Scale 1/50 000

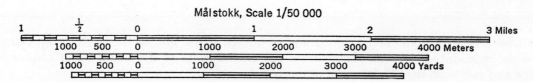

Topografisk kart over Norge

1 / 50 000

Topografische Kaart van het Koninkrijk der Nederlanden

Echelle 1/ 100 000

Carte de France

SCALE 1/62500

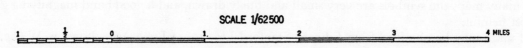

U.S. Department of the Interior. Geological Survey

FIG. 1. SCALE-LINES

SWITZERLAND

SELECTED MAP-SHEETS

Landeskarte der Schweiz 1/50 000   SHEETS—263 WILDSTRUBEL *1960*
                                      264 JUNGFRAU   *1961*

Both these map-sheets cover mountainous country, which includes, especially in the Jungfrau area, great rocky peaks, névés, and glaciers. The Swiss Survey excels in the portrayal of relief, and these maps are outstandingly clear, arresting, and beautiful. This is due to the graphic methods employed in relief representation, the choice and transparency of the colourings, the accuracy and detail of the rock-drawing, and the quality of the printing.

Contours are drawn at 20 m intervals. They are in brown on vegetation-covered slopes, black on rock slopes and screes, and blue on ice and snowfields. Thickened contours are drawn at 200 m intervals and numbers are inset, but though the latter are few, there are numerous spot heights and trigonometrical points. Rock outcrops and cliffs are drawn in black, and areas of snow or ice are left white, with crevasses and other ice features in blue. This results in cooler colours for the heights, and is most effective. In addition, an appearance of oblique illumination from the north-west is obtained by the use of a yellow tint on the vegetation-covered slopes facing north and westward, and a grey tint for all east- and south-facing slopes, which are assumed to be in shadow. Darker greys are used for steep shadowed slopes, but small gradations of tone show up minor details of relief, even on northern and western slopes. The map has thus the appearance of a model, but no detail has been obscured. Water is shown in blue, woods in green, with open woodlands shown by small green circles. Roads (which are well classified), mountain and field tracks, railways, settlements, boundaries, and all lettering are in black. No explanation of the conventional signs is provided at the foot of the map, but most of these are obvious, and a combined characteristic sheet, illustrated with map-extracts, is available for the 1/25 000, 1/50 000, and 1/100 000 maps.

A 2 km grid covers the map face in the 1960 sheet, but this is changed to a 1 km grid in the 1961 map. Grid numbers are printed on the map border, and co-ordinates of latitude and longitude are also given, with the longitude reckoned from Greenwich. At the foot of the map a metric scale-line is drawn, the magnetic variation is stated both in degrees and in grades, and also the datum from which the Swiss Survey determines altitudes. This is the 'Pierre du Niton' in the port of Geneva, and its height has been calculated to be 373,6 m[1] above the average sea-level in the port of Marseilles.

On the reverse of the map-sheet is printed a most useful index diagram of all the 1/50 000 map series.

GLOSSARY
bach—stream. **gletscher**—glacier. **grat**—mountain ridge. **see**—lake. **tal**—valley.

Valley Glaciers: The Grosser Aletsch Glacier

Landeskarte der Schweiz 1/50 000   SHEET 264 JUNGFRAU

It seldom happens that a large physical feature is mapped in its entirety within a single map-sheet of scale 1/50 000, but the whole of the Aletsch glacier (the longest in Europe) and all its tributary glaciers are covered within the Jungfrau sheet. Also included is the long Fiescher glacier, the three highest peaks of the Bernese Alps—the Finsteraarhorn, Aletschhorn, and Jungfrau, and the upper parts of the Lötchen, Lauterbrunnen, and Gastern valleys. It is a sheet of great

---

[1] The Continental method of showing the decimal point has been adopted here.

geographical interest, and shows excellently the beautiful mapping of ice features by Swiss Survey.

Travelling up-valley from the snout of the Grosser Aletsch glacier, the ice-tongue extends for 15 km between mountainous and almost parallel walls. Here there widens the great expanse of the Konkordiaplatz, into which open the snowfields of the Grosser Aletschfirn from the west, the Jungfraufirn and Ewigschneefeld from the north, and the smaller Grüneggfirn from the east. These are the névé fields supplying the glacial ice which feeds the Aletsch glacier itself. Down-valley from the Konkordiaplatz the glacier receives ice only from two small corrie glaciers and one tributary valley glacier—the Mittelaletsch glacier.

None of the great snowfields appear on the map-extract, and only part of the Aletsch glacier itself, but it is hoped that the full sheet will be available for the study of the whole trunk glacier and its tributaries, and of the snowfields that feed them.

THE MAP-EXTRACT

(*Note.* Grid references apply to the kilometre squares.)

The features of the Aletsch glacier (two-thirds of which is included in the extract) are shown in blue, and cover surface levels (indicated by contours), crevasses, surface hollows, streams, and lakes. The depth of the ice and the relief of the valley floor cannot, of course, be read from the map, but the contours of the ice-surface suggest that no marked changes of gradient occur along this stretch of valley. There are no ice-falls or steep ice-slopes, except on the inner curves of the glacier, as it rounds the southern buttresses of the Olmenhorn and the Rothorn. It is clear that the ice-tongue in cross-section is not level, but rises from its margins towards the middle, where it may be 50 m higher than at the sides. This is indicated by the curves of the 2000 m and neighbouring contours, which also bring out its many longitudinal ridges and furrows. Farther up-valley a particularly deep and pronounced longitudinal furrow occurs in the centre of the glacier surface. Marginal crevasses, pointing up-stream, are shown everywhere, and result from the greater speed of flow in the middle of the glacier, and the tensions set up by this in the ice. Longitudinal and transverse crevasses are not so well illustrated, but thousands must occur that cannot be mapped. However, a few examples of longitudinal crevasses are shown in the middle of the glacier where the ice spreads out a little after its constriction in the 'narrows' (647/140), and a great intersection of transverse and marginal crevasses has produced gaping fissures in the steeper slopes where the glacier rounds the Olmen buttress (648/143). It is probable that 'séracs' have been formed here in the broken ice, but they cannot be shown on the map.

The tapering of the glacier to the south shows that it is nearing its end, and only a kilometre beyond the mapped area the snout is reached. Here wastage by evaporation and melting equals the supply of ice pushed down from the valley above. But melting must be considerable over all the ice-surface during the summer days, though the surface freezes in summer nights and in winter all is frozen and snow-covered. This melt-water collects as 'superglacial' streams in longitudinal furrows which act as drainage channels (647/141). The water soon disappears into crevasses or pits in the ice, and temporary pools and lakes of melt-water will drain in the same way. Three small and more permanent lakes are marked (649/145, 647/142), lying in marginal ice carrying a thick load of moraine, and a dwindling remnant of the former large Märjelensee is dammed back behind the wall of ice blocking its valley exit (650/143). A large trough is shown in the glacier surface (648/144), and others are found in the confusion of small hollows and ridges which occur at the junction of the Mittelaletsch glacier and the main ice tongue. They are mapped in fine blue hachures (647/143).

Moraines are composed of rock waste which has either been plucked from the valley walls and floor, or has fallen from frost-shattered slopes above. They are mapped in black, and differentiation has been made between areas strewn with huge boulders and areas or ridges composed of less coarse materials. Obviously the rock waste will accumulate on the glacier margins, and, except at the foot of the Bettmerhorn and of the Eggishorn, the whole Aletsch tongue is fringed with ridges of these lateral moraines.

The most striking moraines, however, are those lying on the ice in the middle of the glacier, following its whole length in sinuous lines parallel to the valley sides. These are medial moraines, and are formed by the joining of adjacent lateral moraines where two glacial tongues converge. This is not illustrated in the extract, but in the whole sheet the convergence of the Oberaletsch

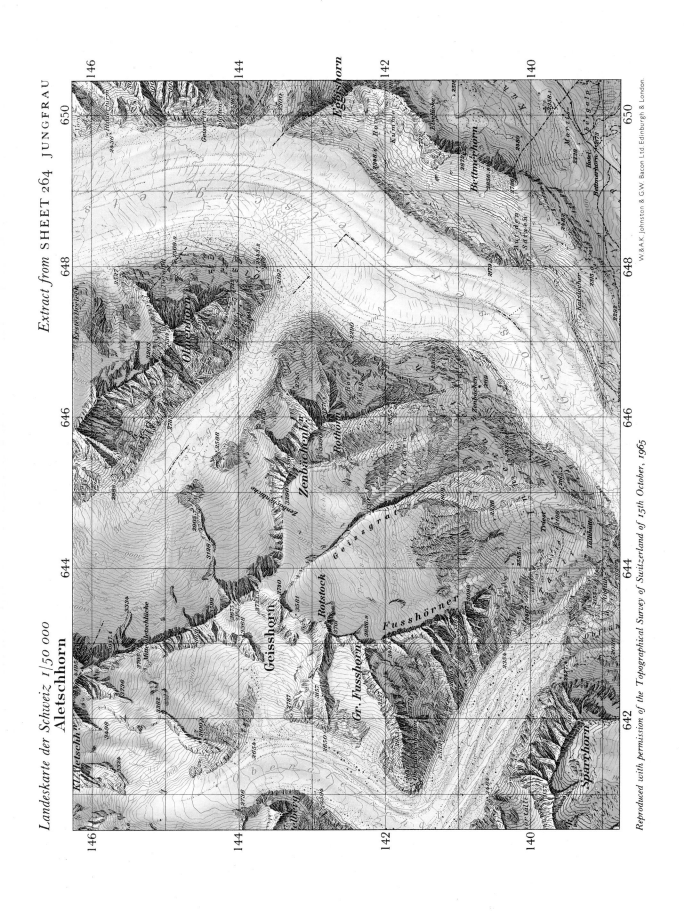

Landeskarte der Schweiz 1/50 000
Aletschhorn

Extract from SHEET 264 JUNGFRAU

Reproduced with permission of the Topographical Survey of Switzerland of 15th October, 1965

W & A.K. Johnston & G.W. Bacon Ltd Edinburgh & London.

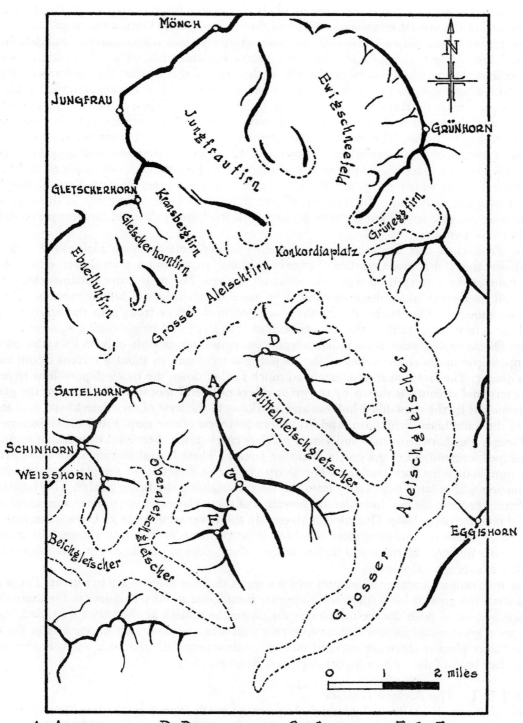

A – Aletschhorn   D – Dreieckhorn   G – Geisshorn   F – Gr. Fusshorn

FIG. 2. THE ALETSCH GLACIER

Heavy black lines mark the mountain ridges which enclose the parent snowfields and
tributary ice-tongues of the Aletsch Glacier. Broken lines indicate the boundaries of the
snowfields and glaciers where these are defined.

glacier and Beich glacier (640/141) provides an excellent example. Some of the medial moraines shown are discontinuous, and some peter out—probably through loss of material in crevasses—and it would seem that the spreading out of the ice below the narrows mentioned above has carried one of the medial moraines outward to the eastern glacier margin (647/139).

The Mittelaletsch glacier is the only tributary glacier to join the Grosser Aletsch within the mapped area. A great semicircle of crested ridges radiating from the Aletschhorn and the Dreieckhorn (just north of our extract) encloses the head of this glacier; the contours on the ice show exceedingly steep slopes, and there are many crevasses and even ice-scarps (644/146). The constant gradient of the ice-slopes does not suggest deeper accumulation of snow in great mountain hollows, and the features of the ice-free southward-facing slopes, north-west of the Olmenhorn, are in keeping with this. Though these have some mountain shelves, there are no corries. The tongue of the glacier thins out noticeably down-valley, and in the steep descent at its valley mouth. Here there are great accumulations of lateral moraine and a confused area of pitted and 'dirty' ice where it unites with the Grosser Aletsch tongue. The appearance suggests that the supply of ice reaching the end of the Mittelaletsch glacier valley is dwindling, and that, if this continues, before long the glacier will fail to make contact with the Grosser Aletsch, but remain contained within its own valley.

The Zenbächen and Triest glaciers are each enclosed between long high ridges from the Geisshorn, and each shows a marked change of gradient, suggesting a central area of accumulation, followed by a steep drop with crevasses and fissures. The melt-water streams which drain them fall over great rocky descents flanked by pronounced ridges of lateral moraine. Curious features, shown by blue hachures, are the elongated oval pits or troughs in the upper parts of the Triest glacier and north of the Zenbächenlücke (644/143 and neighbouring squares).

The Oberaletsch glacier is an independent ice-tongue that extends only to its valley mouth, and opens 480 m above the valley of the Aletsch glacier. From its snout a torrent drains to the main glacier. The fact that it once extended much farther down the rocky slopes—now trenched by its terminal stream—is shown by the great ridges of lateral moraine. The head of the glacier is surrounded by the snow-filled hollows and ice-slopes to the west of the Aletschhorn, and to the east of the Sattelhorn, Schinhorn, and Weisshorn just west of our map. From the Geisshorn and the Grosser Fusshorn two small individual glaciers carry down their load of moraine to add to the heaped longitudinal ridges on the main ice-stream. These lateral moraines are distinctive in their numerous huge rock boulders. The sharp change of direction in the glacier valley marks its junction with a large twin valley from the west, containing the Beich glacier. This junction is interesting because the two inner lateral moraines of these glaciers unite to form the conspicuous medial moraine of the lower Oberaletsch glacier. In this lower section the ice becomes increasingly covered by masses of moraine, some of which is heaped into pronounced ridges. The contours here clearly indicate the ridge and furrow surface of the glacier. Also most noticeable is the large number of superglacial streams.

The map shows a number of features which suggest that the glaciers are in retreat. The supply of ice from the great fields farther north appears insufficient to fill the valleys to the same depth as formerly, or to push the ice-tongues as far down the valleys as they once extended. As we have seen, great moraines now line ice-free valley mouths and mountain slopes, and at the sides of the larger glaciers there are exposed narrow, almost perpendicular rock walls, eroded when the surface level of the ice was higher (642/140, 646/140, etc).

PLATE I   The Aletsch Glacier

This photograph was taken looking slightly east of north from a point some distance south of the Riederhorn, which appears in the middle foreground of the view. The Aletsch glacier is seen foreshortened, and a greater length of it is shown than is included in the map-extract. The main features to note in the glacier itself are its dark-coloured medial moraines and the dark fringe of the lateral moraines on the glacier sides, the steep edges of the glacier tongue sloping down to the valley walls, and the light-coloured eroded band at the foot of these. The two glaciers on the left are the Triest glacier (the nearer) and the Zenbächen glacier (seen almost in profile). Their lower margins of broken ice reach steep cliff exposures, and great abandoned lateral moraines curve around these central precipices. In profile the Zenbächen glacier shows clearly the much gentler slopes of its central area, and its snow surface outlines the southern valley wall of the

Photo : Aerofilms, Ltd.

PLATE I.   The Aletsch Glacier

PLATE II.   Folded rocks in the Gastern valley near Kandersteg

Mittelaletsch glacier, the dark mountain wall behind being the northern side of the valley. The glacier within this valley and all its collecting grounds are, of course, completely hidden. The Aletschhorn towers above all other summits in the top left of the picture, but all the valley of the Oberaletsch glacier is out of view, except its snout and the deposited lateral moraine on its left. This stands out as a pale-coloured ridge against a dark background. Bands of moraine lie on the glacier snout, and make a dark margin to the light-coloured eroded band on the valley wall. The stream flowing from the valley mouth in the middle left is not the entrenched torrent draining the glacier, as the map clearly shows.

In the right foreground extends the Riederalp (over 6000 feet), with its hotels, chalets, and footpaths.

Maps for Further Study

The map-sheets Nos. 263 Wildstrubel and 264 Jungfrau are adjacent, and cover a continuous stretch of mountainous country from the lesser heights around the Ober Simmental in the west to the Finsteraarhorn in the east. Together they give an excellent opportunity of studying the superb representation of relief in the maps of the Swiss Survey.

A Mountain Landscape in the High Calcareous Alps: The Altels District

Landeskarte der Schweiz 1/50 000   SHEET 263 WILDSTRUBEL

The area chosen is a small part of the Bernese Alps, which are themselves included in the High Calcareous Alps. They are composed of intensely folded rocks, mainly of Jurassic and Cretaceous age, and, as the name implies, are mainly limestones, though these have been greatly metamorphosed. During and since the period of their overfolding and overthrusting, the agents of denudation have broken up and removed vast amounts of rock material, so that only sculptured fragments of the folds remain, and the present relief bears no relationship to the original folded forms.

The broken fragments which form the mountains of today are still being attacked and destroyed, and glaciers, avalanches, and streams spread out their debris over the lower ground. The following map-study examines the relief of a very small area, as shown by the map, and notes where possible some of the surface indications of rock structure and some of the deposits of rock waste.

THE MAP-EXTRACT

Five main highland features cross the region roughly from south-west to north-east, and are as follows: the massive Balmhorn-Altels-Rinderhorn group in the south-east; the long ridge of the Gellihorn-Ueschinengrat-Weisse Fluh with its south-westerly extension; rising above this the shorter, higher, and more sinuous ridge of Schwarzgrätli-Felsenhorn-Roter Totz; the Engstligen-grat-Ortelenhorn ridge, continued eastward as a cliff face projecting from the lower slope of the Great Lohner; the Vorder, Mittler, and Hinter Lohner which make up the Great Lohner group in the north-west. Small parts of three deep valleys are also included in the extract area. The Rinderhorn and Balmhorn heights drop by tremendous rock walls (with precipices of over 2000 feet in places) to the valley of the Dala, which flows through Leukerbad a few kilometres south of our area. In the north-east waters from the glaciers of Altels and Balmhorn fall into the Gastern valley, whose river, the Kander, leaves the valley by the gorge of the Klus, to enter the head of the Kandertal. Above the Klus the Kander receives the Schwarzbach, which drains the relatively shallow valley between Altels and the Ueschinengrat, and at the head of the Kandertal it receives the Alpbach, draining the Inner and Aeusser Ueschinen.

The detailed mapping of the great rock face of the Montagne, in the south-east, makes it clear that the rocks of which it is composed are stratified, and that some beds are of greater resistance than others. Below the Rinderhorn projecting beds with almost perpendicular rock faces—presumably of harder rocks—alternate with less abrupt outcrops, and the sharp capping of the

Plattenhörner (614, 615/139) and the Zackengrat (617, 618/140) suggest layers of particularly resistant rocks. The height of this cap in the Zackengrat is marked as 3117,6 m, and the beds can be traced in the rock face at progressively lower levels to the south-west, where, just before the Gemmi Pass, a spot height shows a level of 2286 m. The north-western slopes of Altels and the Rinderhorn also illustrate very clearly the layered sheets that compose the surface of these mountains. A few of these slabs are covered with rock debris, some are ice-covered, but many are steeply inclined, bare rock surfaces. The silhouette of these mountains is striking, with many smooth rock slopes on the north-western side, rising to summits which overlook precipitous drops to the south and east. However, nothing would be further from the truth than to suppose that the structure of these mountains is one of simple inclined layers. The rock face on the northern side of Gasterntal shows that the strata are strongly folded (617/146), and recumbent folds are indicated. Other such folds are shown in the valley walls on the opposite side of the valley. It is clear, then, that the structure of Altels and the Rinderhorn may be one of great complexity of folding and faulting. The surface slabs may be part of an upper or lower limb of a recumbent fold or folds, and the outcrops of the Montagne may be a cross-section of such folds, in which case there would be much repetition of beds in reverse order. Without the information of a geological map it is impossible to do more than to observe the outcrops on the exposed rock faces, but one cannot suppose the mountains to be structurally simple.

The shape of the glaciers and their size would appear to be related to the rock forms. The Balmhorn glacier has its origin in a rounded corrie on the north side of the summit, but there are no rounded corries on either Altels or Rinderhorn. Their glaciers stretch along narrow shelves, or cover inclined rock slabs at the summits. On such inclined surfaces conditions may be too unstable for the development of large glaciers. The southern tongue of the Altels glacier, for instance, appears to maintain its present length as a result of the support offered by the protuberance of 2656 m (selected as a spot height). North of this the glacier does not extend down the steep, slanting rock face anything like so far. The narrow parallel glaciers to the east of Rinderhorn, of which the higher lies about 200 m above the lower, are obviously developed on the projecting step-like shelves of inclined slabs. The small glacier to the south of Altels, and that east of Ober Tatlishorn, lie in similar positions. The largest glacier, the Schwarzgletscher, fed by shelf glaciers from Balmhorn and Rinderhorn, lies in a straight, rock-walled trench, which follows the surface dip of the beds, and cuts deeply into the mountain block, completely separating the eastern and western summits. The deepening of this trench (especially in km square 617/141) seems very great for the size of the glacier, and one wonders whether lines of weakness (such as might result from fault fractures) have aided erosion. (The geological map shows a fault in the Zackengrat a little west of the spot height 3117,6 m, and this fractures the great rock face of the Montagne from top to bottom.)

The cliff faces are exposed to severe frost-shattering, and tremendous accumulations of scree and rock-debris lie at their feet, and roll or are carried down the slopes by rain-wash or by streams. This spread of debris is particularly clearly seen in the Furggentälli and the neighbouring slopes of the Plattenhörner, on the rock faces of the Klein Rinderhorn, and below the Rindersattel, and all the slopes of the Schafberg. The streams deposit their fans or cones of waste at the foot of the slopes of their descent, and the Schwarzbach, draining from the Schwarzgletscher, has built a large cone at the foot of Altels east of the Arvenwald, and a second cone on entering the Gasterntal. Here also the Geltenbach and streams from the Balmhorn glacier have deposited large fans, and pushed the Kander to the other side of the valley. Some of these fans appear very porous, for in four cases streams have disappeared, as their waters seep into the gravels. The Gelten fan is marshy, but the higher cones of the glacier streams and the Schwarzbach carry forest. However, the trees here are scattered, though forest is continuous on the Gastern valley floor.

There is probably much morainic material strewn over the Spittelmatte and the Gasterntal, but it cannot be recognized as such. However, clearly marked lateral moraines border the Schwarzgletscher, especially on its right-hand side, and these continue far below its snout. Much of this material must be washed down and form part of the Schwarzbach cone and the gravel banks in its braided course.

The Gellihorn-Ueschinengrat-Weisse Fluh ridge is also composed of steeply inclined strata, as is indicated on the eastern slopes facing the Klus, and the scarp slopes which are situated

612   614   616   618

148

Holzberg
Niunhn
2200 *Bonderjrunde* 2089
1896 *Bergli*
Ryharts
Gernst Born
Eggen
schwand
1196.6
1977
2276
Lohner S.A.C.
2171
2930 *Hint Lohner*
Aeusser
1725
1348
1504
1297
1481
2099
2284
Weite Kumme
3003
Ueschinen
Balmen
1635
2055
1549
1356
Schafberg
2154.5
Jägerdossen
1833

146

Mittl Lohner
2287.1
Gellihorn
Stock
1856.4
2284.2
1355
Waldhaus
Gastern holz
1367

2048.4
Vord Lohner
N 2358
1755
Auf der Egg
2333
Winteregg
1700
1428
Gasterntal
1390

Inner Ueschinen
2445.9
Leimern
1960.5
Langenboden
2264.3
1907.2
Lärchi
2269.3
2497.4
Unt. Tatlishorn
2436
Bise

144

2735
Ortelenhorn
2551.4
Ortelen
1861
Unterbächen
1964.5
Spittel
matte
1875
2159.7
2961
2840
2658.9
ungelochtigh
2090
arven
1929
Ob. Tatlishorn

2398.3
Weisse Fluh
247
wald
1901.6
Sagiwald
2656
2651
2857
Tschalmeten
2399
2184
2406
Altels

142

Felsenhorn
2782.5
2087.6
Kl. Rinderhorn
2200
2208
2959
3418
3629
Balmhorn
2061
2072.5
Schwarenbach
2915.1

2628.3
2466
2297
2340.5
Rinderwasti
3120
2700
3117.6
2869
Roter Totz
2840.1
Seestuts
2229.7
2500
Rinderhorn
3454
3236

140

2900
Daubenhubel
2415.7
2807
2223
2570
Blankhorn
2650.3
2220
Fluhkap.
2067
Lämmern
2527.1
2468
platten
2344
Genmipass
2639
Roter Totz
2052.9
Fluhalp
2039
2300
2318
Daube
2314
Clawinenalp
2038.3
2458

138

612   614   616   618

Reproduced with permission of the Topographical Survey of Switzerland of 15th October, 1965

north of Weisse Fluh show clearly an alternation of hard and softer beds. The crest of the ridge at Gellihorn is noticeably sharp, with cliff exposures on both the eastern and the western sides, and the strata here are obviously very steeply inclined indeed. Screes are banked at the foot of the eastern scarp, and spread out to the Spittelmatte. The far more gradual slopes of the west have some covering of soil, and probably of vegetation, but are broken by the outcrops of the uptilted strata. There are no inclined bare rock faces, as are found on Altels. The complete absence of streams on any part of the ridge suggests that the rocks of which it is composed are permeable. Softer rocks appear to outcrop below the eastern cliff face, but when traced south-westward both of them disappear under surface deposits, and other thicknesses of hard and perme-able rocks are exposed in the Lämmernplatten, and in a long shelf northward, and also in the inclined platforms leading to the Gemmi Pass. Ice has certainly travelled the valley of the Gemmi route, and a glacier has probably over-deepened the hollow in which lies the Daubensee. However, the north shore of this lake suggests that the rock barrier may be incomplete, and that the dam near the point 2229,4 is formed of moraine or rock waste. The old outlet channel is followed for a time by the road, and becomes almost a small gorge before reaching a second basin filled by a smaller lake. Whether this is dammed by rock or by deposits is not clear. A pronounced step ends this upper part of the valley, and its second section has more regular walls, and a far less rocky floor. This may be basically of softer and less permeable rocks, and is certainly covered by many deposits. The braided river keeps close to the eastern wall, and some of its waters, seeping from its cone below the Schwarzgletscher, appear to be obstructed, possibly by moraine, as small lakes and marshes have been formed. At its precipitous descent into the Gasterntal the river, in a narrow rocky gorge, has cut through hard layers which underlie the valley at some depth.

The Schwarzgrätli (613/143)-Felsenhorn-Roter Totz ridge is possibly related to the Engstligen-grat and its continuation northward, though the nature of any relationship is not clear. While the eastern scarps of the Felsenhorn and Roter Totz are steep, the more gentle western slopes dip beneath the Täliseeli, and probably also beneath the Üschinentäli glacier, and outcrop farther down the valley as a semicircle of cliffs. These cliffs continue northward for some distance, jutting out of the scree-covered valley side, below the continuation of the Engstligengrat. The two outcrops may be just the harder rock layers of a continuous series, or they may be repeat outcrops in a section of a small recumbent fold, or related in one of many other ways. The map just records their presence.

The Inner and Aeusser Ueschinen valley must have been ice-filled at one time, and the valley has some glacial features, though it is not typically U-shaped, and has a flat floor only in its upper section above Unterbächen. The river Alpbach flows at the foot of the western slopes of the Ueschinengrat, and has cut a steep course, which at the valley mouth lies 300 m above the floor of the Kander valley. The lack of tributary streams on the right-hand side of the valley has already been noted, but the gentler slopes on the left would appear less permeable, as a number of streams arise below (and a few above) the resistant outcrops. Much scree covers the lower slopes, and there is probably some moraine.

Three structural features appear recognizable in the great Lohner Group. All the highlands of the mapped area have remarkably few streams, but a number of streams and deep gullies occur on the western slopes of this mountain group, with a spring-line of about 1800–2000 m. We have noted that springs arise at this level on the eastern side of the mountains, and it is possible that less permeable beds completely underlie a permeable summit. At greater altitudes steeply inclined beds build the western slopes of the Vorder Lohner, but they do not appear elsewhere, and they may be a different series or differently inclined from those that build the summits farther east and north. There is some evidence of faulting on the eastern rock face between the Mittel and Vorder Lohner, where the thick basal outcrops appear to have been considerably displaced.

Only the lower end of the Gasterntal—a perfect example of a glacial trough—is included in our region. Its river, the Kander, after a braided course down the flat valley floor descends the 130 m to the head of the Kandertal in the narrow ravine of the Klus.

Two Geological Sections across the Area from South-south-east to North-north-west

It is obvious that any topographical map on the scale of 1/50 000 can do no more than give some of the facts of surface relief, and that this in turn can only here and there reveal features

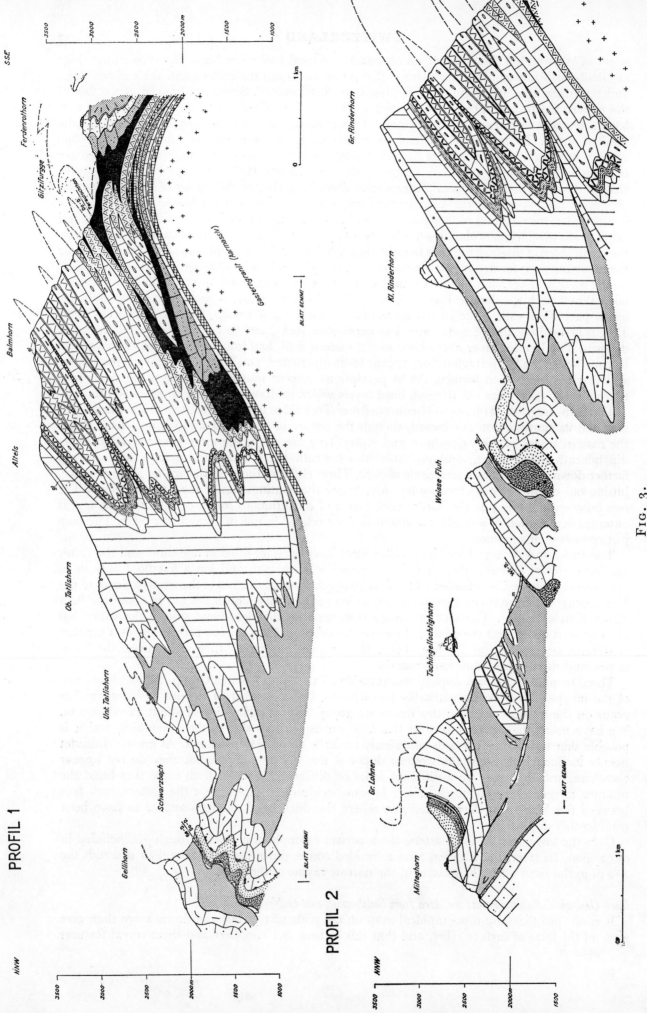

PROFIL 1

NNW

SSE

3500
3000
2500
2000 m
1500
1000

Geilihorn   Schwarzbach   Unt. Taltishorn   Ob. Taltishorn   Altels   Balmhorn   Ob. Tatlishorn   Glizifürgge   Ferdenrothorn

Gasterngranit (Karmess N)

— BLATT GEMMI —

3500
3000
2500
2000
1500
1000

1 km

PROFIL 2

NNW

3500
3000
2500 m
2000
1500

Millteghorn   Gr. Lohner   Tschingellochtighorn   Weisse Fluh   Kl. Rinderhorn   Gr. Rinderhorn

— BLATT GEMMI —   — BLATT GEMMI —

1 km

Fig. 3.

H. Furrer, reproduced from "Blatt 473 Gemmi, Erläuterungen", with permission of the Swiss Geological Commission

of surface structure, disclose a glimpse of geological detail, or give a hint of rock character. How much is revealed must also depend upon the skill of the cartographer. The maps of the Swiss Survey show beautiful mapping of rock forms and faces, and an outstandingly clear and detailed representation of relief.

The geological structure of this region is summarized in the Gemmi Sheet (1/25 000) of the geological Atlas of Switzerland, and described in the explanatory text accompanying the sheet. Both map and text are the work of the Swiss geologist, Dr Heinrich Furrer, and part of Profiles 1 and 2 are reproduced here from his text with his permission. The profiles are reproduced in part only, and are reduced in size. The key has been greatly simplified, as Dr Furrer's text is far beyond the scope of this study. But it is hoped that the simple descriptions which follow will enable the student to make use of these profiles, which reveal the underlying structure of the region.

PROFILE 1 (*See Fig.* 3)

This profile or section cuts across the mapped area from south-south-east to north-north-west, passing through the Balmhorn and Altels summits, the Ober and Unter Tatlishorns, and the Gellihorn. Its direction is transverse to the folds. The profiles show the great complexity of overfolds and overthrusts to the north-west, and the key to the diagrams indicates that the area is composed mainly of Jurassic and Cretaceous rocks.

The intensity of the folding in the Middle Jurassic beds that build Balmhorn and Altels is clearly illustrated. The recumbent folds are pressed one upon another, greatly crushed and distorted, and some layers are completely squeezed out. The great cliff face of the Montagne cuts through the folds, and the same beds may outcrop a number of times in confusing succession. Note that some beds (flinty limestones) are evidently harder than others, and protrude in the cliff face.

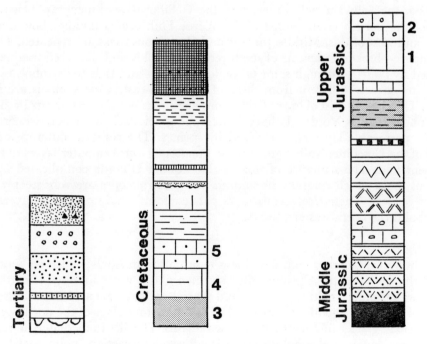

KEY TO FIG. 3 (greatly simplified)

H. Furrer, reproduced from "Blatt 473 Gemmi, Erläuterungen",
with permission of the Swiss Geological Commission

5. *Hauterivien-Kieselkalk*   2. *Tithonien-Portlandien*
4. *Valanginienkalk*   1. *Kimeridgien*
3. *Valanginien-Berriasien*

Younger Jurassic limestones (*Kimeridgien*) build the summit of Altels and its north-western slopes. Although vertical lines distinguish these beds in the profile, they are folded in the same way as are the beds of Balmhorn. And this means that in this line of section the north-western slopes of Altels correspond closely to the slope of the inclined beds of the upper limb of a recumbent fold. The succeeding resistant limestones of the Upper Jurassic (*Tithonien-Portlandien*) compose the Ober Tatlishorn and its north-western slopes. Softer Cretaceous rocks (*Valanginien-Berriasien*), which include argillaceous schists, overlie these limestones, appearing around the Unter Tatlishorn and underlying the Schwarzbach valley. These schists are of course folded and faulted in accord with all the other rocks of the series, but the all-over shading chosen to distinguish them gives the profile greater simplicity and clarity. The Schwarzbach has cut deeply into the compact limestones (*Valanginienkalk*) which follow these schists, and right through the upper limestone (*Hauterivien-Kieselkalk*). In this line of section, therefore, the Schwarzbach valley has rocky outcrops on both sides, and, owing to the folding, similar outcrops compose much of the north-western slope and the isolated summit of the Unter Tatlishorn.

Thin, highly folded bands of Tertiary rocks follow the limestones, and the series is then cut short by one of the thrust planes of the region. All the rocks of the Gellihorn region have been thrust forward from the south-east, and are the remains of overfolds.

To the west of the thrust plane the same Cretaceous beds are repeated, the schists and marls forming the gentle slopes at the base of the Gellihorn, and the compact limestones, very sharply uptilted, outcropping in the crest of the Gellihorn, its eastern cliff face, and its long, dry western slope.

PROFILE 2 (*See Fig.* 3)

This longer section extends from the Grosser Rinderhorn through the summit of the Weisse Fluh to the Mittaghorn (300 m north of the western boundary of the extract). From the Grosser Rinderhorn westward to the Weisse Fluh it bears a great resemblance to Profile 1, and the two sections together supply a clear indication of the structure of the Altels-Balmhorn-Rinderhorn mountain mass, the Schwarzbach valley, and the Gellihorn-Ueschinengrat-Weisse Fluh ridge. At the foot of the north-western slopes of the Weisse Fluh occurs another boundary, a second thrust plane, and west of this, Middle Jurassic and Cretaceous rocks are repeated. The structures are most complex—broken remnants of small recumbent folds and shattered fragments of larger folds separated by faults. Although some of the formations—and thus the symbols used to distinguish them—are slightly different from those of the south-east, some symbols are immediately recognizable. The clayey schist of lower Cretaceous age (folds not shown) occurs in the Ueschinen valley, and underlies the Vorder Lohner, outcropping on its eastern and western sides, and forming a less permeable layer characterized by springs. The resistant outcrops on the north-western wall of the Ueschinen valley are Jurassic limestones—broken outer layers of the remnants of a recumbent fold. The structure of the Vorder Lohner is made complicated by faults, but the Cretaceous rocks which compose its summit and eastern slopes are very steeply inclined, in places almost vertical. These Cretaceous rocks pass conformably into thinner layers of Tertiary rocks which build the north-western slopes.

Ice Fall from Altels

Dr Furrer, in his explanatory text, describes the ice-fall from Altels, which on September 11th, 1895, buried the Spittelmatte Alp and killed six men and a great number of cattle. Following a summer in which much melting of snow and glacial ice had taken place, a large part of the glacier plunged down the smooth and steeply inclined limestone slabs of the north-western slopes, leaving only a small glacier fragment which now remains. This lies immediately to the south-west of the track of the ice-fall, and is held up by a small rocky projection (point 2656).

PLATE II Folded Rocks in the Gastern Valley near Kandersteg (opposite p. 15)

This photograph, taken from the southern wall of the Gasterntal, looks down to the Waldhaus lying in a small woodland clearing on the valley floor, with the braided Kander behind. The foreground of the view is not included, but it is probable that the photographer was standing near the point 616,8/145,2, above the gorge of the Schwarzbach. The opposing rock face shows a most striking series of folds, some recumbent, in thick, resistant Cretaceous strata. The harder

PLATE III. Gellihorn and the head of the Kander valley

Photo: Kandersteg Tourist Office

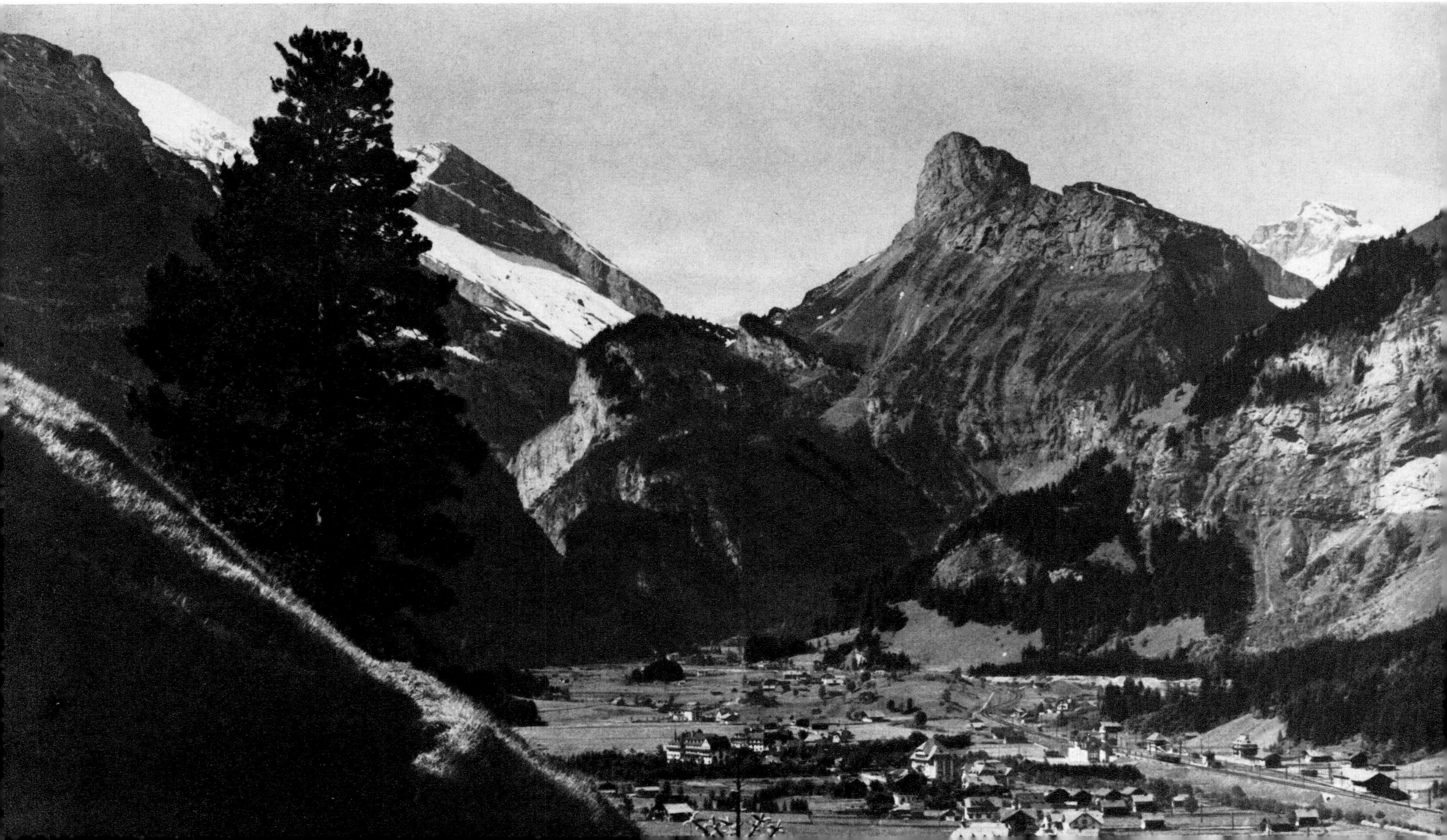

Photo: Aerofilms, Ltd.

PLATE IV. *Above :* The Puy de Dôme from the South-east

Below : View from the northern slopes of the Puy de Dôme

Photo: Paul Popper, Ltd.

beds have been thrown into high relief by erosion along bedding planes and the decay of interbedded layers of softer rock. Great screes have collected at the foot of the valley wall, composed
of coarse fragments, with a characteristic steep angle of rest.

Jagerdossen is prominent on the skyline above the shadowed western slopes, and behind these,
in the far distance, a small part of the eastern Kander valley appears, with above it the peak of
Birre. The higher peak on the right of Birre is the Zahlershorn, which is outside the area shown
on the map-sheet.

PLATE III   Gellihorn and the Head of the Kander Valley (opposite p. 20)

This view looks southward to the head of the Kander valley from a point on its eastern wall
a little distance north of Kandersteg. The Kandertal is a large and typical glaciated valley, with
flat floor and very deep sides, though the lower parts of the western wall are hidden by tree-
covered screes.

Rising immediately above the valley head is the Gellihorn, built of hard limestones, with its
uptilted strata clearly shown. To its west the river Alpbach drops over a steep descent from the
Ueschinen valley, but this river cannot be seen in the view, as it is hidden by the western valley
wall. To the east of the Gellihorn the land drops with an irregular slope to the Schwarzbach
valley, at the foot of the Tatlishorn and Altels mountains. Here is the route to the Gemmi Pass,
and a footpath to this leads up from the Kandertal head and around the eastern side of the
Gellihorn. The smooth snow-covered rock slabs of the Tatlishorn and Altels slope north-westward,
and are partly hidden in the photograph by a large fir-tree. Below them the south-west wall of
the Gasterntal, above the Klus, is brightly illuminated by the morning sun, though the Klus
itself is difficult to distinguish.

The beautifully situated tourist centre of Kandersteg has grown considerably since this photograph was taken.

Map for Further Study
Geological Atlas of Switzerland 1/25 000 SHEET GEMMI (No. 32)

Although this map is of especial use to the advanced geologist, there is much that can be of
help to the student. Individual outcrops can be related to the relief, as shown in the map-extract,
while extensive areas of superficial deposits covering lower mountain slopes and valley floors are
shown in great detail.

FRANCE

SELECTED MAP-SHEETS

Carte de France 1/50 000 (Type M)   SHEET XXV—31 CLERMONT-FERRAND
partially revised 1959

Carte de France 1/50 000 (Type 1922)   SHEET XXXVII—17 SÉLESTAT
partially revised 1960

Carte de France 1/100 000   SHEET M—22 MONTPELLIER *1957*

Three of the map series of France are illustrated in the sheets selected. The hachured maps (Type M) have been derived by the enlargement of an older 1/80 000 series, and are being gradually replaced by the sheets of Type 1922. Much of France has been covered by this newer series, but there are still many areas (including Clermont-Ferrand) for which the only 1/50 000 map is of Type M. This sheet has been selected because it illustrates the use of hachures, and covers a landscape of unique interest. The conical puys and spreading lobes of lava lend themselves well to portrayal by hachures, which are here drawn in black and combined with brown contours at 20 m intervals. Numbers are inset in every hundredth contour, which is more heavily drawn, and there are also many spot heights and trigonometrical points. Although hachures give a graphic representation of relief, it is obvious that they can obscure other detail, especially on steep slopes, though in these sheets they may have been coarsened by enlargement.

Other colours of the map are a green overprint for woodlands (heavy and somewhat obscuring), blue for water areas, and bright orange for main and secondary roads (the colour broken for secondary roads and narrower main roads), and a superimposed 1 km grid in purple. Cultural features such as narrow roads, railways, buildings, vineyards, orchards, and field boundaries are in black, as are also administrative boundaries and lettering.

There is much marginal information, including many conventional signs, a list of abbreviations, scale-lines, detailed instructions for obtaining a grid reference, and a diagram to show true north, grid north, and magnetic north, with the magnetic variation given in degrees. Most of this information is given in English as well as French.

The Sélestat map-sheet (Type 1922), published in 1939 and partially revised in 1960, illustrates the present standard 1/50 000 map of France. It is a clear map, with a restrained use of colour. There are no hachures, but contours (which are not numbered) are shown in brown at the smaller interval of 10 m, with strengthened contours at 50 m intervals. In special areas where slight changes of gradient are significant contours are inserted at 5 m intervals. In addition an oblique illumination is suggested by a soft grey tint on eastern and southern slopes, giving a good plastic impression of relief. However, the green tint employed for forests, with numerous forest paths heavily drawn in black, is very dominant, and on this sheet somewhat obscures the relief. Much information on the landscape is given, including field tracks and hedges, vineyards and orchards (in black), and rivers, mill-streams, and marshes (in blue). Considerable use is made of abbreviations, and some of these are reproduced below, with a few of the symbols used.

Marginal information includes a selection of the conventional signs, a scale-line, and a diagram to show magnetic north, with the magnetic declination expressed in grades and centesimal minutes. Co-ordinates of latitude and longitude are given, with the longitude measured in degrees from the Greenwich (International) Meridian, and in grades from the Paris Meridian.

The 1/100 000 Montpellier sheet (published 1957) is an example of the new series on this scale, which completes coverage of France in 1967. It has many features of similar type to those of the present 1/50 000 series, but as it is largely used as a route map, roads are very clearly shown in red (main roads) and yellow (secondary roads). Kilometre distances between towns, and between marked road stations, are printed in red alongside the routes to which they refer. Marginal information includes a list of symbols. In this sheet vineyards are mapped as fine green dots, brushwood and bushes in diagonal green lines, and woods in finer diagonal green lines.

ABBREVIATIONS

Carr^e	Carrière	Quarry	R^{au}	Ruisseau	Stream
Ch^{au}	Château	Castle	R^{er}	Rocher	Rock, crag
Fab^e	Fabrique	Factory	R^{ne}	Ruine	Ruin
Fil^{re}	Filature	Spinning-mill	Sanat	Sanatorium	Sanatorium
F^{me}	Ferme	Farm	S^{ce}	Source	Spring
F^{ne}	Fontaine	Spring, cistern	Sc^{ie}	Scierie	Sawmill
F^t	Forêt	Forest	Teint^{rie}	Teinturerie	Dye-works
M^{ln}	Moulin	Mill	T^{ie}	Tuilerie	Tile-works
M$^{on Fre}$	Maison Forestière	Forester's Lodge	T^r	Tour	Tower
Pts	Puits	Wells	Us^{es}	Usines	Works, factories

SOME SYMBOLS 1/50 000 MAP TYPE 1922

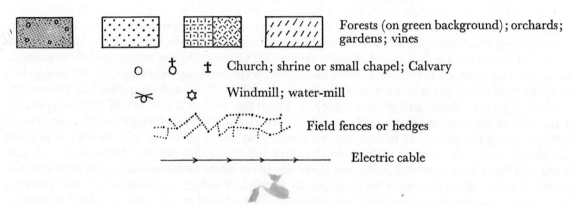

Forests (on green background); orchards; gardens; vines

Church; shrine or small chapel; Calvary

Windmill; water-mill

Field fences or hedges

Electric cable

Volcanic Landscape and Fault Scarp: Clermont-Ferrand

Carte de France 1/50 000 (Type M)   SHEET **XXV**—31 CLERMONT-FERRAND

THE MAP-SHEET

This sheet is of special interest, as it covers part of one of the most distinctive areas of the high Auvergne Plateau and of its sharp eastern edge, and to the east of this area a strip of the Limagne depression and a short length of the river Allier. The town of Clermont-Ferrand and its suburbs is also completely covered.

The Auvergne Plateau lies here about 780 m above sea-level, and from its surface rises a multitude of small extinct volcanoes. These volcanoes, or *puys*, are strung out in a succession of small groups parallel with the eastern scarp of the plateau, and with the main cones about 4 or 5 km from it. The puys not only vary in size, but differ greatly in form, in age, and in the materials of which they are composed. Although long extinct, they still appear astonishingly fresh. All have suffered long-continued denudation, which has partly destroyed some of the cones composed of softer materials—scoria, ashes, cinders, etc.

Many of the puys are typical volcanic cones with circular summit craters, worn and broken in some cases, and in others perfectly shaped (Puy de la Coquille, Puy de Jumes). Other puys have double craters, second cones having developed within the older craters in later eruptive phases (Puy de Côme). Some older puys are half ruined, probably as a result of paroxysmal eruptions far back in their history which destroyed their cones, leaving broken ramparts— remnants of calderas—within which new craters were later formed (Puy de Pariou). Many of the puys are partly formed of lava, which has streamed from them over the plateau in great lava-flows called *cheires* or *cheyres*. These can easily be distinguished on the map, and there are a host of examples, such as those that flow westward from the Puy de Louchadière and Puy de la Coquille, from the north-west of the Puy de Côme, or westward from the puys Balmet and Fillu. But these fluid lavas were not extruded from all the volcanic vents of the plateau. In close proximity to volcanoes surrounded by such lava-streams are others which extruded lava so viscous that it congealed almost immediately, forming dome-like structures without craters (Sarcoui, 9873). As the outer layers hardened any further extrusions from the vent exerted pressure from within, cracking the surface and enlarging the dome by expansion. The Puy de Dôme was probably formed by highly viscous lava filling the crater and plugging it from within by the growth of a summit dome.

The lava-flows and the materials washed from these volcanoes (over 30 cones within the mapped area) have covered much of this part of the crystalline plateau with thicknesses of porous rocks, into which surface waters readily percolate. The map shows the dry, rugged, and broken rock surfaces of many of the cheires, covered with scanty brushwood. However, forest growth appears to be on the increase here, as the 1/100 000 map of this area, published in 1962, shows far more wooded areas than are represented on this 1/50 000 map, published in 1952, and many of the cheires, the target-practice areas, and the shooting-ranges now appear to be largely forest-covered (Champ de Tir de Ceyssat, Cheire du Puy de Côme). On the margins of these volcanic rocks, and especially on the borders of the lava-flows, water wells up in springs, or can be reached by shafts, and many permanent streams arise. The availability of water-supplies has determined the sites of plateau farms and villages (9167, 9177, 9179), and in a number of these—especially in the east of the region—water-mills are also marked, indicating a former use of water-power (9163, 9167, 9266, 9279). It is unlikely, however, that these mills are still in use; it is more probable that electric power is utilized for the small industries that persist. Decomposed volcanic debris and lavas form very rich soils, and there are many areas between the line of puys and the eastern plateau edge which must be prosperously farmed. A village occurs at nearly every stream source (and these are very numerous), and others have developed at wells and springs. Settlements are seldom more than 2 km (1·2 miles), and often only 1 km, apart, yet the region is 700–800 m above sea-level (2000–3000 ft.), and winter snow is persistent. This considerable farming population would not be drawn to this rigorous region unless it had something to offer.

The eastern margin of the plateau is most clearly defined, even though tongue-like terraces and flat-topped buttes project from it into the Limagne plain. The sharp line of demarcation between the high plateau (over 750 m) and these terraces and buttes is a sudden steep drop from well over 600 m to 500 m, forming a conspicuous wall which is generally wooded. Its continuity is hardly broken by a succession of deep valleys, as these do not cut into the plateau for any distance, but climb immediately to its surface. The character of this sharply cut edge, coupled with the volcanic activity, suggests that the plateau has a fractured margin, and that along a line of faults there has been either uplift of the plateau or subsidence of the plain, or perhaps both. To the south of Royat (0367) an old volcano, Gravenoire, actually straddles the plateau edge, and its lava-flows extend to Beaumont and far beyond. Although lava-flows are not named as such on the map, their tongue-like projections from the plateau are so distinctive that they can easily be recognized. Other obvious examples are seen at Volvic, both north and south of Sayat, and north of Nohanent. Volvic, in fact, lies on a lava-flow from the Puy de la Nugère, and its houses are built of basalt from the great quarries (clearly marked on the map) on the northern slopes of the mountain.

Thermal and mineral springs often accompany volcanic activity in a faulted region, where earth movements have taken place, but there is little evidence of these on the map. But they occur widely, at Clermont-Ferrand, at Durtol, and at Royat, which is a famous spa. However, two sanatoria are shown, and they are most probably associated with the medicinal value of some of the springs. One is at Monteyre (0174), south of Chanat, and the other at Durtol (0371).

The buttes, rather lower than the plateau, are shown by the contours to have flat summits and steeply descending slopes. Their structure is not discernible from the map, and it is only the Chateaugay butte, closely related to lava-flows from the plateau, that even suggests that they are the remnants of basalt flows or other volcanic rocks, capping and protecting underlying rocks of less resistance. These softer and less resistant rocks once filled the Limagne valley, but have been eroded from its surface. Note how the plateau streams hug the sides of both lava-flows and buttes, closely outlining them, and by their erosive action (both now and in the past) increasing their

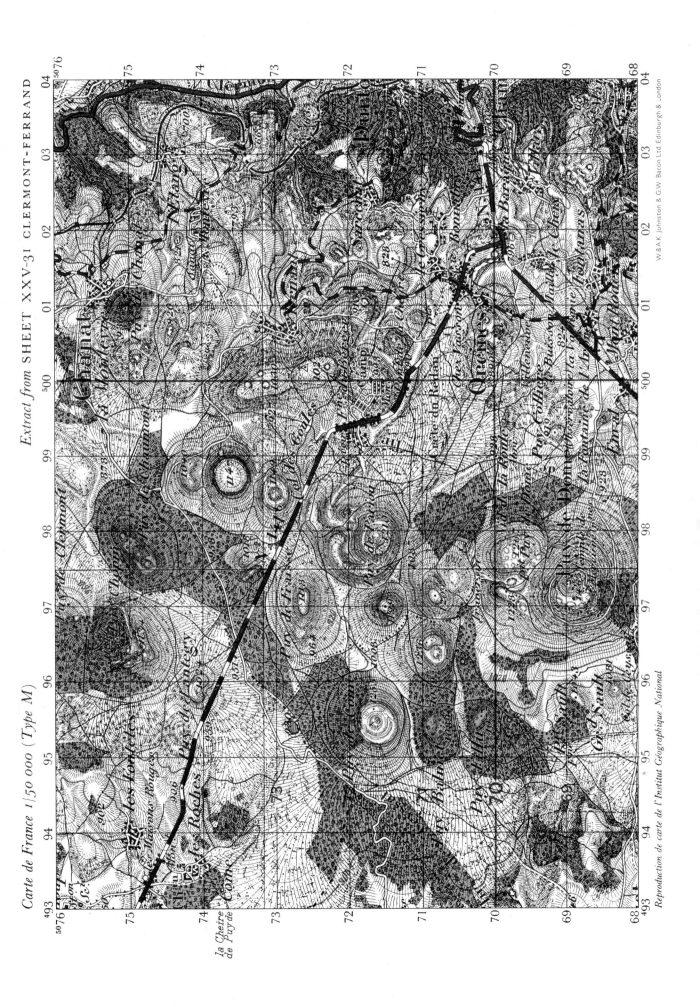

Carte de France 1/50 000 (Type M)

Extract from SHEET XXV-31 CLERMONT-FERRAND

Reproduction de carte de l'Institut Géographique National

W & A K Johnston & G W Bacon Ltd Edinburgh & London.

altitude relative to the plain, so that though once poured out over the Limagne surface, they now stand up as relief features.

Only a small part of the southern region of the Limagne plain is included in the mapped area. Its floor lies at about 320–330 m, though it is interrupted by a number of isolated hills. Everywhere it is cultivated, and vineyards cover many of the sunnier hillsides and lower ground, while orchards are widespread. No special symbol distinguishes any other crop, but the numerous large, compact villages, as well as numbers of dispersed farms, bear witness to the fertility of the region. The plain is watered by many streams from the plateau, all draining east and north-east, presumably to join the Allier farther down-stream. But the number of reservoirs suggests that, lying in the lee of the plateau, it may be in a rain-shadow area.

Clermont-Ferrand lies at the foot of the plateau, with the butte of the Côtes de Clermont rising steeply to the north, and the terraces and hills which ascend to the great butte of Gergovia closing it in on the south. Only to the east is it open to the plain. Its site must have made it an important market and exchange for plateau and plain products, and an important distributing centre. It is at the centre of a web of routes, of which the north-south route, passing through the old town of Riom and following the Limagne south (No. 9), and the east-west route linking Lyons and Bordeaux (No. 89) are outstanding, and probably of long history.

The town centre, with an important church or cathedral within an open square, is situated on a hill summit of 407 m. From this centre it has spread down gentle slopes to stream valleys on both north and south, covering them with massed buildings. The town is the Prefecture of the Department of Auvergne, and has therefore administrative importance, and it is also an industrial centre, with enormous factories and industrial works spreading to the east. (Though unnamed on the map, these are the rubber-manufactures and tyre-works of Michelin.) Around the town open suburbs have climbed the lower slopes of the hills, but several closely packed and grimly designed housing estates have been built to the east and south. To the west Clermont is linked with Royat, where the tiered terraces must have splendid views. The Mont Ferrand arsenal and the Aulnat aerodrome lie on its eastern outskirts, where they open to the plain.

There is little indication of the settlement's long history, though Roman ruins are marked (0567), and the remains of a Roman temple of Mercury lie on the Puy de Dôme summit. Gergovia must have had pre-Roman importance as a stronghold of ancient Gaul.

THE MAP-EXTRACT

The selected extract includes examples of most of the main features of the plateau and its eastern edge, but it does not cover any part of the Limagne. Attention has already been drawn to the double craters of the Puy de Côme and the Puy de Pariou, and to the rounded dome of Sarcoui, 1147 m (9873), and the more lofty dome of the Puy de Dôme. Immediately south of Sarcoui is the simple crater of the Puy des Goules, 1149 m, though like Sarcoui this cone is not named on the map. Some care is needed in interpreting the mapped summits of the puys. The hachures are not always simple to read, but contours and spot heights in conjunction with the hachures reveal the surface forms. In mapping the contours of the Puy de Côme and Puy de Pariou arrows have been drawn across the 'depression contours' to show the descending slopes of the crater hollows (that of the Puy de Pariou is partly obscured by lettering). The towering, craterless Puy de Dôme dwarfs all the other puys, and from its northern slopes a wide panorama of their lesser summits is obtained. A road spirals up to this viewpoint.

The lava-flow from the eastern side of the Puy de Pariou with its sharp ridge—the Crête du Redan—is shown in its entirety, but only a small part of the great cheires in the west of the mapped area are included. The Cheire du Puy de Côme extends for $5\frac{1}{2}$ km, as does that from the Puy Balmet. Not only is their stony nature clearly shown (note the village of les Roches, 9374), but also the steep edges of these thick lava-tongues. In some places such tongues converge, creating a barrier and forming a depression by enclosure, in which water is trapped to form a lake. An unnamed example of such a lake is seen north of the Puy de Côme (9572). Although the cheires are now more wooded than shown here, even on the more recent map they are still marked as great shooting-ranges (Champs de Tir), and the presence of a military camp (9971) is probably related to this. Reference has already been made to the agricultural population of this area, and the extract shows fifteen settlements on the spurs and valleys between the line of puys and the eastern edge of the plateau, and nine of these are situated at 800 m or over.

The plateau edge is wooded, and falls abruptly from over 640 m to 500 m, the main road at its foot crossing and recrossing the 500 m contour as it traverses the lava-flows and terraces that flank the edge. This is cut by the deep valleys of five streams and a number of smaller ravines. All these valleys are very short and steep, and their streams are swift torrents. The source of the longest at Ternant (0072) is only a little over 3 km from the plateau edge, and the stream rising at Chanat (0175) falls from 800 m to 500 m in 2½ km.

PLATE IV (opposite p. 21)
(a) The Puy de Dôme from the South-east
This view is easily correlated with the map, because of the clear boundaries of the forest. The distant plateau stretches westward beyond the mountain, but the view does not include the group of puys to the north.

(b) View from the Northern Slopes of the Puy de Dôme
This is a hazy photograph, but it is valuable because the contrasted shapes of the smaller puys are readily recognizable. The outer rampart of the Puy de Pariou, the circular crater of the Puy des Goules, and the rounded dome of Sarcoui lie, one behind the other, on the right. The broken ramparts of the Puy Chopine lie directly in front of the ruined Puy de Louchadière in the left background. The beautifully formed Puy de Côme is not included in this view.

Maps for Further Study
1. It is assumed that the full 1/50 000 sheet will be available for study.
2. *Scale 1/100 000 SHEET L—16* CLERMONT-FERRAND
   A beautifully clear map published in 1962, which includes:
   The southern Limagne plain;
   The western scarp and the projecting buttes from the scarp edge;
   The Montagne de la Serre (classic example of inversion of relief);
   The whole string of puys with good examples of cheires;
   A large lava-dammed lake (Lac d'Aydat).

The Vosges Border near Sélestat

Carte de France 1/50 000 (Type 1922) SHEET XXXVII—17 SÉLESTAT

THE MAP-EXTRACT
This area has been chosen because its landscapes, though very limited in extent, include so many of the features typical of the eastern borderland of the Vosges and the adjoining valley floor. The Rhine does not appear, as it lies too far east, and the Vosges mountains are here of small stature, but their steep eastern margin, their well-cultivated lower slopes, the terraces at their feet, the *ried*, and the forest of the plain are all represented.

This fringe of the Vosges is of very moderate height, with the highest summit of 662 m rising above Dambach. The mountains are covered with forests to their summits, though some rocky outcrops occur among the trees (Rocher de Falkenstein and others). However, the map gives no clue to the nature of the rocks or to the character of the forest trees. The eastern slopes facing the rift-valley are seen to be dry, but the mountain area of the extract is too small to bring out the contrast between this scarcity of streams and the abundance of surface water elsewhere in the Vosges. The full map-sheet shows that each of the numerous and deep mountain valleys (*gouttes*) has its swiftly flowing torrent (*bach*) which feeds the small but powerful Vosges rivers, the Giessen and its tributary, the Lièpvrette. These rivers unite within the gap which trenches the Vosges border shown in the mapped area, and have deposited an easily recognizable fan of sediments on entering the plain to the east.

The mountain forests are seen to be well controlled, and carefully preserved. Forestry stations

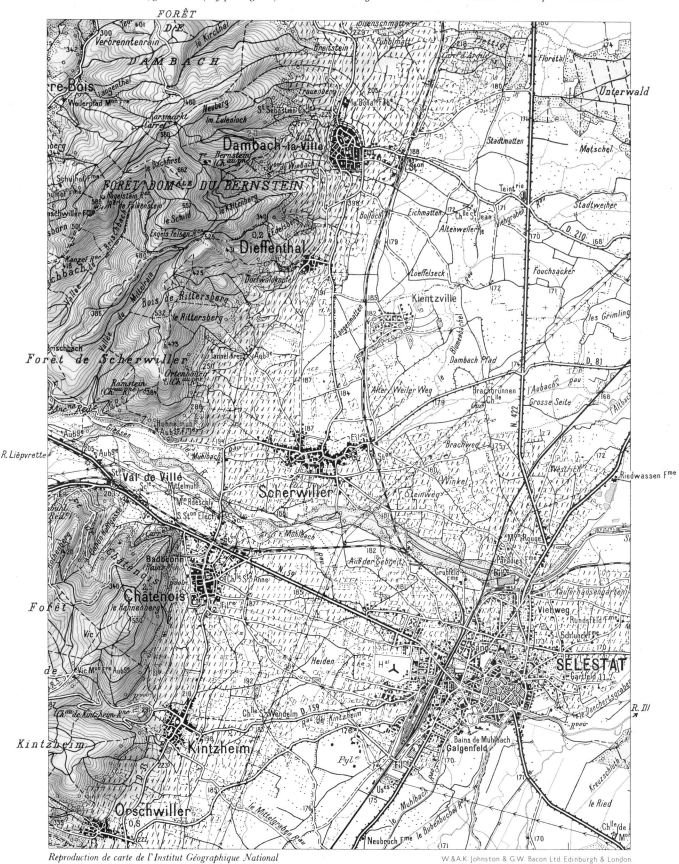

are marked, and the forest tracks and rides are so numerous that no part of the forest is difficult of access. Much of the forest shown is the property of the local town and village communities, and the named forests of Dambach, Scherwiller, Châtenois, and Kintzheim lie wholly or partly within the extract area. The forests of Sélestat and Orschwiller lie just beyond the boundaries of our area. Many domanial forests, such as the Forêt Domaniale du Bernstein, are now under State control, but the ruined château of Bernstein still exists. Three other ruined châteaux are perched on forested spurs far above the sloping vineyards.

The upper eastern slopes of the Vosges are seen to be exceedingly steep, and from the Hannenberg, above Châtenois, this abrupt descent falls uninterruptedly to 250 m. However, farther north, beyond the Rittersberg, the descent is broken by many irregular spurs in which the contours indicate marked changes of gradient. Around and above Dieffenthal and Dambach this is especially marked, and suggests that rock outcrops of differing character and resistance occur. All the slopes are conspicuously dry, and would appear to be permeable. The small river above Kintzheim is the only surface stream to cross the slopes, and even this disappears above the village to reappear 1½ km farther east. Vosges water must seep underground, as a number of springs issue at the base of the slopes—below Orschwiller at 220 m, west of Kientzville at 188 m, and at Dambach above 200 m (the exact position of the spring is not shown). The map shows that whatever the underlying structure may be these dry slopes spread out into a terrace flanking the mountains. This varies greatly in width, and has no clearly defined eastern margin.

Linked with this terrace, and thrusting out as a great lobe into the plain, is the slightly raised fan of the river Giessen. The Ill is directed eastward by the southern spread of this fan, and on the low bluff overlooking the river a short length of the old walls of Sélestat still remains. The Giessen crosses its fan in a strip of woodlands and no settlements approach its banks, but a smaller stream, with waters derived partly from the Giessen and partly those of the Mittelrain, flows across the northern part of the fan and passes through the small town of Scherwiller. A southern Vosges stream, independent of the Giessen, flows across the southern part of the fan to Sélestat, but its course, like that of the Kintzheim river, is not traced on the map through the built-up area.

Everywhere the dry lower slopes of the Vosges are covered with vineyards, and the easterly and south-easterly aspect and protection from wet westerly winds makes this a particularly favourable site. The rainfall must be adequate, as there is no indication of any form of field irrigation, though there are reservoirs on the mountainside above three of the terrace villages. The vineyards extend from the slopes to cover the terrace at their foot, and are often interspersed with orchard trees and gardens, which are especially numerous near its lower margin. Above Dambach-la-Ville vines reach a height of over 350 m on the sheltered southern sides of spurs and spread over the terrace eastward for over 3 km, descending to under 180 m to the south of the little hill of Plettig. Elsewhere the vineyard belt is narrower, but it spreads widely over the whole of the Giessen fan and even descends to heights of under 170 m, linking up with the vineyards of Kintzheim, Châtenois, and Scherwiller in a great expanse of intensively cultivated land.

It is probable that the string of small towns along the Vosges slopes owe their prosperity, if not their existence, to the vine. The expansion of the vineyards and the tremendous growth of the wine trade with Flanders, Switzerland, and Germany in the late Middle Ages greatly enriched this region, and were responsible for a remarkable density of population along the eastern mountainsides. Sélestat has a position which is similar to that of the larger and more important Colmar, and which offers obvious advantages as a centre of exchange for the products of the plain, the Vosges borderlands, and the mountain valleys. Its routes penetrate into the heart of the Vosges by means of the Giessen and Lièpvrette valleys, and it must have shared the prosperity resulting from the wine trade of the rift-valley routes. Its crowded nucleus, with the site of its former walls clearly distinguishable, is surrounded by modern and more open growth, and it has obviously shared in the industrial development of Alsace. Two spinning-mills are marked, and unspecified 'works', but there are certainly other industries than those shown, for Sélestat has important manufactures of metal wires and tissues. Dambach-la-Ville is still almost completely contained within its walls, and the map shows that three of its roads enter the town through gateways. Medieval in its plan, and probably in some of its buildings, it lies embedded in vineyards which reach up to its own forest-lands. But like its neighbours, Châtenois (whose walls have gone) and Scherwiller, it has added some industrial activity to its viticulture, and each of these small towns has a factory on its outskirts. The old cotton or the newer textile industries of Alsace are represented by the spinning-mills (Fil^re) marked in Châtenois and Scherwiller, but also marked are the dye-works (Teint^rie) away from any settlement but on the main road east of Dambach, and the tile-works (T^le) just within the mapped area south of the Giessen. As one might expect, sawmills (Sc^le) have been established in this forested country, and are marked with accompanying water-mills on the Muhlbach in the Val de Villé. The five water-mills shown here indicate clearly how great a part direct water-power once played in this area, but it is most unlikely that these mills still function or even exist. The network of power-lines indicate the modern use of electric power, which is highly developed in the Vosges area.

As we have seen, the Giessen, with the waters of the Lièpvrette, has deposited a great spread of sediments on the floor of the plain. This extends right across the mapped region. To its south lies part of the flood-plain of the Ill and its tributaries, which is named 'le Ried'. The marshland of the Ill and Rhine flood-plains is known as ried, but here the ditches indicate that, though subject to floods, the area is partially drained. A tree-lined road and some field paths cross it, and trees border some streams, but there are no hedged enclosures. A fragment of forest occurs just within the map boundaries, and is part of the extensive Illwald. It is interesting to note from the full sheet that this forest lies on slightly lower ground than the ried, and is intersected by as many drainage channels. East and north of the raised Giessen fan stretches a larger area of the Ill flood-plain, crossed by many tributary streams but fewer drainage channels. No marshland occurs actually within this ried area and the land may have been fully reclaimed. Meadow areas (*matten*) are marked, and orchard trees, hedges, and a number of field paths suggest a cultivated land. But this is not a land of dispersed population, and only one isolated farm is marked—Riedwassen Farm. In the north-east of our area, as in the south-east, there is just included a small part of a larger forest. This is the Unterwald, which covers slightly higher ground. The full map-sheet shows this is the first of a long line of wooded areas which lie west of the Ill and parallel to it.

A Note on the Structure of the Vosges Border near Sélestat

Within the mapped area the Vosges are composed of granite, with a summit covering of Carboniferous and Permian rocks in a very small part of the extreme south-west. There is no Triassic sandstone here, though this forms a horizontal capping over many of the summit areas outside the extract boundaries. The mountains are bounded on the east by faults, and fall in abrupt escarpments to about 350–400 m. Here a series of step-faults, with successive downthrows to the east, results in outcrops of progressively younger sedimentary rocks. These form the lower Vosges slopes and the low hills at their feet. The rocks are of Secondary and Tertiary age, and include as well as the Triassic sandstone already mentioned, a Triassic limestone (*Muschelkalk*), soft marls and harder oolites of the Jurassic, and some of the older rocks of Tertiary age. Beside these step-faults, there is another series crossing them at a wide angle, cutting up these younger sedimentary outcrops into blocks and wedges, and causing much diversity of detail in the Vosges border. The faults may in some places bring about a juxtaposition of softer and harder rocks, and differential erosion has produced gentle slopes on the Jurassic marls and steeper slopes or low hills in the more resistant limestones. In some places, however, there are no abrupt changes of gradient as the faulted border is crossed.

Borings have shown that the Secondary and Tertiary rocks are continued beneath the floor of the rift-valley, which is covered by Quaternary deposits. These consist of vast quantities of fluvio-glacial sands and gravels, carried down from the great Rhine glacier of the Ice Age, which advanced as far as the present river's entry into the rift-valley. These sands and gravels have been cut up into parallel terraces by the Rhine and Ill and their tributaries. Their permeable character has resulted in forest growths, while the alluvial flood plains of the rivers (which are subject to inundation) are in places ill-drained and marshy. These are the rieds; though many of these areas in the Ill valley have now been drained and cultivated. The Quaternary loess, which has covered the terraces close to the Vosges foothills, has given these an extremely fertile soil.

It is obvious that only the eastern fringe of this rift-valley is included in the map-extract, but its features are related to the pattern described.

In the centre of the mapped area the valley deposits have been overlain by the mass of river sediments brought down from the mountains by the Giessen and its tributaries.

PLATE V.

Gates of Dambach-la-Ville

Photos: Margaret E. Wood

These views show two of the three ancient gates of this small and wall-enclosed town of medieval origin.

Above: The southern gate from within the town, and one of its old streets. The names of some of these recall a town life of the past—Rue des Marchands, Rue des Tonneliers, Rue des Boulangers, Rue des Forgerons.

Below: The main eastern gate as seen from without the town walls. It is dated MCCCXXIII. Behind the town are seen the lower slopes of the Vosges.

PLATE VI.   Aigues-Mortes

Maps for Further Study

1. The full *1/50 000 map-sheet Sélestat* should be studied. Beyond the map-extract there is much industrial development around the Andlau and Kirneck rivers in the north, and this has also developed along the narrow Lièpvrette valley west of Sélestat. The wider Giessen valley is less industrialized, and many vineyards have spread up its south- and east-facing slopes. Note the compact nodal settlement of Villé, the plan of which suggests that it was once walled.

2. *Sheet 1/100 000 R—9 Colmar*

Sélestat is very well placed in this sheet, which gives complete coverage of a small part of the Rhine rift-valley from the Vosges to the Black Forest. It illustrates many typical features of this valley, including:

The Rhine channels, its forests and rieds;

The Ill valley and its stretches of ried;

The parallel strips of forestland;

The Vosges border and foothills, the latter particularly clear between Sélestat and Colmar;

The Lièpvrette and Giessen valleys as in the 1/50 000 map;

A clear presentation of the distribution pattern of large villages and towns;

The similarity of position between Sélestat and Colmar.

This is a most valuable sheet.

References

(i) An excellent summary of the regions of the Rhine rift-valley, with accompanying sketch-map, is given in E. Juillard, "Une carte des formes de relief dans la plaine d'Alsace-Bade".

(ii) An account of the Vosges borderlands from the Sélestat region to the south of Colmar, with sections drawn to scale from the Vosges scarp to the rift-valley floor, is given in J. Vonfelt, "La bordure vosgienne entre Sélestat et Rouffach".

(See Suggestions for Further Reading)

Delta Landscape: Aigues-Mortes

Carte de France 1/100 000   SHEET M—22 MONTPELLIER

The enormous load of gravels, sands, and silts carried by the Rhône and its Alpine and Cevennes tributaries has been deposited in the tideless Mediterranean Sea to form a large, arcuate delta. At the head of the delta, 40 km from the sea, the main river divides into two branches—the western Petit Rhône and the eastern Grand Rhône, enclosing between them the Ile de la Camargue and the vast Etang de Vaccarès. Since the middle of the nineteenth century the main flow of the river has followed the course of the Grand Rhône, and its deposits have resulted in a great advance of the delta to the south-east, while deposition at the mouth of the Petit Rhône is now hardly sufficient to balance the erosive action of the marine currents.

Delta channels (unless dyked) tend to change their courses, especially in times of flood, and parts of former channels of both of the Rhône branches remain in the delta. The Vieux Rhône, lying west of the present course of the Grand Rhône, is part of an abandoned channel, and is marked in the 1/50 000 map, as are fragments of a former more westerly course of the Petit Rhône. In distant times the delta had three river arms, and on one of these (now completely obliterated) Aigues-Mortes was built. Traces of generations of old delta distributaries remain, and though they have long since been abandoned, their old levees (called *lônes*) still exist as slightly raised ground, composed of fine alluvium. These form the higher lands of the delta, and are cultivable, and provide sites for farms and for roads. Between them is a series of enclosed marshy basins, which were once lagoons, but which through countless years have been filled with flood deposits and blown sands. They are all impregnated with salt, and though some areas are sterile, the marshland vegetation of others supports herds (*manades*) of half-wild black bulls and the white horses of the Camargue.

The strong coastal currents, sweeping from east to west, and strengthened by the force of south-easterly winds, have carried much delta material westward, but the quantity of sediments deposited by the Grand Rhône is such that it continues to build its long headland eastward, in spite of the erosive action of these currents. However, farther west the old headlands formed by abandoned river arms are blunted and shortened, while the shallows between them are cut off from the sea and converted into lagoons by sand bars and spits. On these the winds pile up great sandhills.

THE MAP-EXTRACT

The extract region is divisible into two parts—a section of the Languedoc plain in the north and the extreme westerly fringe of the Rhône delta in the south, with a dividing-line between them roughly corresponding to the course of the Canal-du-Rhône-à-Sète.

Approximately half the northern section is agricultural land devoted almost exclusively to vineyards, while the rest is largely marshland with some improved areas. The marshlands are very low-lying, and reach only 0·4 m at a distance of 2 km from the Etang de l'Or and north of Aigues-Mortes. They were probably formed in coastal waters, which were long ago cut off by the westward extension of the delta, and filled with silt. They are very scantily peopled, but five small and compact settlements and a scattering of large farms (mas) show a moderate population in the vine-covered plain. This rises gradually to the north, reaching altitudes of 5 m and 7 m, and the full sheet shows that the area is bordered by a half-ring of low, dry hills. On the 1/50 000 map-sheet these are named les garrigues. A number of water-courses cross the plain, but most of them do not carry a constant flow of water—a reminder of the extreme heat and drought of the Mediterranean summer. Such streams are shown by sinuous pecked lines—e.g., la Viredonne Ruisseau near Lansargues. However, three permanent rivers maintain a southerly course.

The Vidourle (flowing from the border of the Cevennes) is the largest, and its winding course has been straightened below St Laurent-d'Aigouze, and is shown on the 1/50 000 map to be enclosed within embankments, and its flow controlled by dams and weirs. The Canal de Lunel is the canalized course of a small local river, and in the east much of the water of the Vistre has been diverted into the Vistre Canal and its linked channels. Disconnected lengths of its former course, the Vieux Vistre, still remain in the marshes. The Canal-du-Rhône-à-Sète probably follows the former course of at least one of these rivers, as two short cut-offs are shown to the south of the canal between the Etang de l'Or and Aigues-Mortes, and two others are drawn on the larger-scale map. These and the little delta peninsulas at the head of the Etang de l'Or suggest that some of the waters of the Vidourle, and also of the Lunel, may once have drained westward into the lagoon. The rivers clearly do not follow their natural courses, and channels have been constructed from them all, by which their fresh waters are connected with the network of ditches in the reclaimed salt marshes. However, while many of the marsh ditches hold permanent water, some are seasonally dry.

The map-extract gives no indication of the utilization of these obviously reclaimed lands, but the 1/50 000 map marks a bergerie on the farm le Destrech, and so indicates that the area was (or is still) used as sheep pasture. Formerly sheep from the Alps were grazed on the delta marshlands in vast numbers during the winter, when the Alpine pastures were covered in snow—one of the classic examples of transhumance—but this has greatly declined, and it is probable that these reclaimed lands are now used more profitably. The 1/50 000 map also shows considerable lands under rice-cultivation in the Vistre marshlands. This occurs along much of the Vistre valley, from its northern limit in our region to beyond the mapped railway, and also in one small area in the west, south of the Mas de Tamerlet. As the advance of rice cultivation has been most spectacular in all the delta, it may now have spread greatly here.

The south-eastern region of the mapped area, though it does not include any section of the two present Rhône distributaries, has examples of most of the typical features of the delta lands. Four landscapes dominate this region—the slightly raised and cultivated lands, dotted with farms; the extensive and almost uninhabited marshes; the great expanses of salt lagoons; the long lines of sand-dunes and sandspits bordering the Mediterranean.

The higher lands stretching from east to west behind Aigues-Mortes, about 2 m in height and now vine-covered, are the old levees (lônes) of a former channel of the Rhône, now completely obliterated. This broad ribbon of higher ground provides a route between the marshes, and

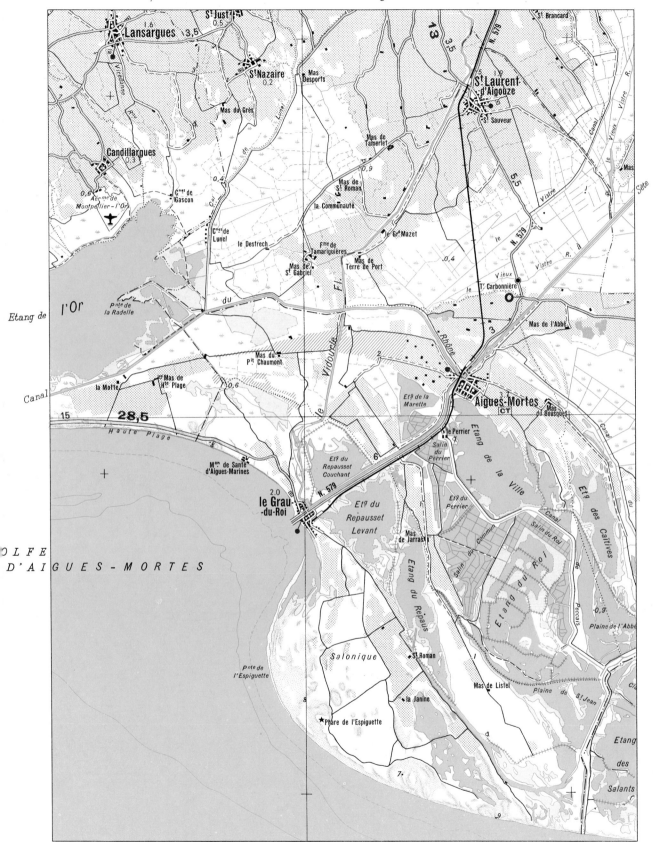

supports a number of farms. Similar lands stretch south-east from Aigues-Mortes. Much younger abandoned channels of the Petit Rhône occur in the extreme south-east of our region. The canal between the Etang des Salants and the Plaine de St Jean follows the old course of the river, and two of its branches are named on the 1/50 000 map. The 'Rhône-mort' can be traced south of the Etang du Roi, and, more southerly still, the channel of the 'Rhône de St Roman' is clearly distinguishable. The strips of cultivated land bordering these channels may be their old levees.

The extract also includes the western margins of two of the great marshes of the delta. They lie in depressions north and south of the higher ground of Mas de l'Abbé. These marshes spread eastward, and the full sheet shows that each of them encloses a large *étang*, and that they fall almost, or actually, to sea-level. Though the difference between this and the height of the levees may seem trifling, in the delta it is of vital significance. The depressions were once sea lagoons, and it is probable that both marshes and étangs are salty, and possible that the marsh vegetation provides only rough pasture. In the small part of these depressions included in the extract no settlements are marked, but there appears to be some reclamation, and it is possible that this may have made rapid progress since the map was published (1957), and that the region has now some excellently farmed rice-fields.

The wide spread of étangs to the south are either completely enclosed by younger levees, or cut off from the sea by great sandspits, which have blocked their former openings (*graus*). Their waters are both shallow and salt, and the salt content is increased by the tremendous evaporation in the heat and drought of summer. As the waters dry up, the exposed shores can become encrusted with salt in some areas, and this has resulted in a salt industry which has persisted throughout the delta for centuries. The basins of evaporation (*salin*) are clearly shown and named on the map.

The coastal fringe of the area reflects the westward sweep of the shore currents. The smooth curve of the Pointe de l'Espiguette is prolonged in the elongated sandspits and beaches that are in process of cutting off from the sea a stretch of coastal water. Le Grau-du-Roi—the only opening in the coastal barrier within the mapped area—is artificial, and protected from silting by its long breakwaters. Westward the sediments have built a smooth shore which continues beyond the map as a narrow sandspit. (This is shown in the full sheet to extend for over 20 miles in a great south-westerly sweep to Sète, cutting off the Languedoc coast from the sea, and enclosing great lagoons.)

The winds, too, have played a part in fashioning the coast, and the dunes are heaped up to greater heights than are attained anywhere else. It is clear that the vine has been established in some of these sandy areas. The inner section of the Salonique may be composed in part of old levees, but the sandy nature of most of it is obvious, and yet vineyards extend to the midst of the dunes, and back the narrow Haute Plage beyond le Grau-du-Roi. The discovery that vines planted in such sandy areas are rendered immune from Phylloxera has made possible the utilization of districts once considered worthless.

It is obvious that the sweep of coastal sediments has directed former Rhône channels westward, and finally choked their outlets. The Vidourle also has no natural outlet to the sea. Its distributaries form a small maze of channels before entering the Maritime Canal, which joins Aigues-Mortes and le Grau-du-Roi. Seasonal étangs to the west (shown in pale blue) and fingers of marshland to the east suggest that a small delta once existed here, but the course of the river is now partially controlled, and embankments prevent its waters from entering the Etang du Repausset Couchant.

The coastal road and the Maison de Santé are slight indications of developments which have probably proceeded further than the map suggests. The tourist possibilities of the Haute Plage and the refreshment provided by this empty land are now increasingly recognized.

PLATE VI Aigues-Mortes (opposite p. 29)

Aigues-Mortes has grown little since it was built in 1240 to provide a port of embarkation for a fleet of vessels, to carry an army of St Louis to the Crusades. It was then in natural contact with the open sea, to which the lagoon on which it stood gave access by means of an opening through an ancient shore-line. But at the end of the sixteenth century the sediments of the Petit Rhône had silted up many of the lagoons and the sea openings, or *graus*, and the town gradually ceased to operate as a port. The preservation of its complete walls, gateways, and towers, and also of its original street pattern, gives it a peculiar interest. There has been some growth of the town to the north, beyond the walls, but this is not enough to destroy its striking medieval appearance. It stands now, as it has stood for over 700 years, complete, sun-baked, and solitary, beside its shallow lagoon. To-day it is linked to the sea by the Maritime Canal, and westward to Sète and eastward to the Rhône by the Canal-du-Rhône-à-Sète. The former canal is seen bordering the sun-illuminated west wall of the town, and again in the right background, and the latter canal is seen in the central foreground, and continues under a bridge to the left. Some of the many vineyards which surround the town are shown to the left of the canal in the foreground and beyond the eastern walls on the left. Just in front of the viewer, and to the right, a garden of small crops (possibly early vegetables) is protected by high, parallel hedges, planted as windbreaks against the force of the mistral, a violent north wind.

The muddy floor of the Etang de la Ville, half seen through the water, and the peninsulas fingering into the lagoon are both characteristic of the delta, as are the 'salines' shown in the extreme right background. These are enclosed basins, where trapped waters evaporate and leave behind encrustations of salt. A considerable area of these is shown on the map, and the district has been important for the production of salt for centuries.

The railway-line follows the canal to le Grau-du-Roi, and the trucks at the station and the barges on the canal indicate that the Aigues-Mortes of to-day is not without some commercial activity.

Maps for Further Study

The whole sheet M-22 Montpellier includes a most interesting stretch of the Languedoc lagoon-coast linking le Grau-du-Roi and Sète. This sheet and the adjoining 1/100 000 sheet N-22 Arles together cover the whole delta of the Rhône.

The following 1/50 000 sheets fill in much detail omitted from the 1/100 000 maps, particularly of rice-cultivation and further land reclamation: Sheets XXVIII—43 Lunel and XXVIII—44 le Grau-du-Roi.

Reference

For a most valuable and interesting account of all factors concerned with rice-cultivation in the Camargue, see J. Bethemont, "Le riz et la mise en valeur de la Camargue" (see Suggestions for Further Reading). Although this paper deals specifically with the Camargue, much of the information applies equally well to the region of the map-extract.

GERMANY

SELECTED MAP-SHEETS

Landesvermessungsamt Baden-Württemberg

1/50 000 (Normalausgabe)	SHEET L 6516 MANNHEIM *1960*
1/50 000 (Schummerungausgabe)	SHEET L 7522 URACH *1964*
1/25 000	SHEET 8324 WANGEN-WEST *1961*

Each of the largest states, or *Länder*, of West Germany has its own Survey Department and publishes its own maps, and the three following extracts have been chosen from the maps published by the Survey Office of Baden-Württemberg. They are completely representative of German maps as a whole, as all the Surveys publish standard map-series of similar scale and style.

The two 1/50 000 sheets have been chosen because they show different methods of representing relief, and also cover very contrasted landscapes. The Mannheim sheet (Normal Edition) has no hill-shading, but the Urach sheet (Hill-shaded Edition) achieves a modelled effect by the use of a pale yellow tint on northern and western slopes and a grey tint on southern and eastern slopes. In both editions brown contours, with numbers inset, are drawn at vertical intervals of 10 m, and interpolated contours, shown in broken lines, are freely used to reveal minor features of reliefs, such as small ridges in the Rhine flood-plain, or shallow depressions in the Alb surface. Although the contours are lightly drawn, they are very clear. Finely drawn symbols distinguish a wide range of other landscape features, which include cliffs and other rock outcrops, 'dolines' or sinks, caves, pits, prehistoric barrows, excavations, and quarries. Although small, these symbols are clearly distinguishable.

The Urach sheet, which covers a mainly agricultural region, illustrates the considerable detail of land utilization which is shown. Tree symbols are small and well-chosen, and outside the transparent green overprint representing woodland areas they are most accurately placed, as are roadside trees. These, as well as moor, grazing-land, orchards, gardens, vineyards, and hop-fields are shown in green. Only in the 1/25 000 maps are we told that uncoloured areas represent arable land.

The naming of the landscape features is very well placed throughout the whole Urach sheet—easily read and yet unobtrusive. Much information as to the status of the small towns and villages is indicated by the style and size of the letterings used, but no explanation of this is given in the many conventional signs which appear in the map-margin.

The Mannheim sheet illustrates the mapping of a large urban and industrial area. The large built-over city blocks are shown in solid black, and so are the industrial works and factories. Smaller buildings and blocks, separated by gardens or open spaces, are drawn individually, and the gardens appropriately coloured. All roads are either shown automatically in white, as the city blocks are blacked in, or they are distinctly drawn. There emerges a most informative urban plan, in which the congested city centres and the industrial areas are clearly distinguished from the main residential regions and suburbs. This sheet was chosen partly because of the most interesting design of Mannheim's inner city, but also because its mapping is an example of superb draughtsmanship. Names are few, and placed well outside the built-over areas, even in some places too far from the districts to which they refer.

The 1/25 000 map-sheet Wangen-West can be compared with the Ordnance Survey maps of the same scale. Two points alone will be mentioned here. The contours, drawn with a vertical interval of 10 m, with numerous form-lines of 7·5 m, 5 m, 2·5 m, and even 1 m, give a most exact representation of small relief features, and the drumlins are beautifully portrayed. Much accurate detail of land-utilization is also shown, with forest cover, pasture, and marshland marked by symbols and arable land left blank. Hop-fields, vineyards, orchards, and gardens are also clearly distinguished.

Marginal information, especially of the 1/50 000 sheets, is very detailed, and a good map catalogue (*Kartenverzeichnis*), which provides map indexes and small illustrative map-extracts, is obtainable from the Survey Office in Stuttgart.

It is worth noting that the German datum *Normalnull* is the mean sea-level of the North Sea as gauged at Amsterdam (NAP—*Nieuw Amsterdams Peil*).

GLOSSARY

bad—swimming-bath. **graben**—ditch, trench. **fels, felsen**—crag(s), cliff(s). **freilichtbühne**—open-air theatre. **heide**—heath, moor. **höhle**—cavern, grotto. **holz**—copse. **jägerhaus**—game-keeper's house. **loch**—hole. **maar**—crater. **moor, moos**—bog, peat-bog. **torfgrube**—peat-pit. **wald**—forest, woodland. **weiher**—pond, fish-pond. **weiler**—hamlet. **ziegelhütte**—brick-kiln.

ABBREVIATIONS

A.P.	.	Aussichtspunkt	viewpoint	Kgr.	.	Kiesgrube	gravel-pit
Br.	.	Brunnen . .	spring	Kläranl.	.	Kläranlage	filter plant
Dom.	.	Domäne	domain	Schl.	.	Schloss . .	castle
El.W.	.	Elektrizitätswerk	power station	Schiessstd.	.	Schiessstand	shooting-range
Fbr.	.	Fabrik . .	factory, works	S.M.	.	Sägmühle	sawmill
Grabh.	.	Grabhügel .	tumulus, barrow	Wbh.	.	Wasserbehälter	tank, cistern
H.Hs.	.	Hütte, Haus .	hut, house	Whs.	.	Wirtshaus	inn
Kap.	.	Kapelle . .	chapel				

SELECTED SYMBOLS

1/50 000

Moor with isolated trees and bushes

Meadow and pasture

Vineyards

Hopfields

Gardens

Parks

Orchard, with or without meadow

Chimney or smoke-stack

Rampart, barrow (tumulus)

Cavern or cave

Quarry, pit, or excavation

Doline or earth subsidence

1/25 000

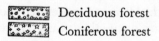

Deciduous forest
Coniferous forest

Drumlin Landscape near Lake Constance

Landesvermessungsamt Baden-Württemberg. Topographische Karte 1/25 000
8324 WANGEN-WEST

During the Ice Age great valley glaciers extended northward from the cover of ice over the Alps, and spread out fanwise in vast lobes over the Tertiary deposits of the pre-glacial lowlands. Southern Württemberg (Oberschwaben) and Bavaria are covered with the moraines left by these glaciers, and with the terraces of gravels and sands washed from them by fluvio-glacial streams. In the Lake Constance area the Rhine glacier spread as far north as the Swabian Alb in an

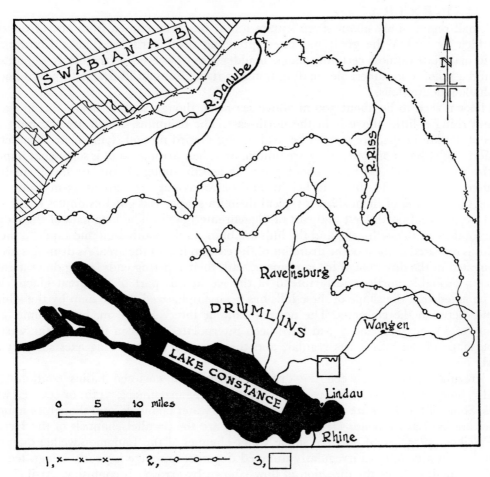

FIG. 4. SKETCH-MAP OF THE GLACIAL DEPOSITS NORTH OF
LAKE CONSTANCE

Based on E. de Martonne

1. Northern limits and traces of terminal moraines of the Riss glacial period
2. Northern limits and traces of terminal and recessional moraines of the Würm glacial period
3. Approximate area of the map-extract

enormous fan. The moraines are not all of the same age, as there were four periods of glaciation separated by warmer interglacial periods, and it is the moraines of the last two glacial periods which form the fans in the Oberschwaben region of Württemberg. The older moraines are those left by the glaciers of the Riss glaciation, and the younger and less extensive moraines, forming an inner fan, are those of the last ice advance in the Würm glaciation. The characteristic forms of the older moraines have been obliterated by erosion, but those of the last glacial period are still fresh and clear, and terminal moraines, recessional moraines (marking stages of retreat), and drumlins are clearly recognizable. Beyond the terminal moraines extensive terraces of outwash gravels and sands occur.

The terminal moraines of the Würm glaciation form a low watershed, separating the streams draining across the terraces to the Danube from those draining across the ground moraines and drumlins to Lake Constance and the Rhine. (See Fig. 4.)

THE MAP-EXTRACT

This small region (only about seven square miles) has been chosen from one of the drumlin areas which lie within the great moraines spreading northward from Lake Constance. The morainic materials (almost certainly much boulder clay) have been irregularly deposited, and they build a relief of innumerable small hummocks rising from an ill-drained uneven floor, with many shallow depressions.

This floor is seen to lie about 500 m above sea-level, though slightly below this in the south-west, and rising a little above it in the north-east. The drumlins, which are the most striking features of the landscape, are seen to be oval or egg-shaped mounds lying close together. Some may stand singly, but more often they are united, and their arrangement is somewhat haphazard. Their size varies, the largest being about 750 m in length, though many are much smaller, and they range from 511 m to 566 m in height, and on an average rise about 43 m above the surrounding floor. Many of them show a typical drumlin shape, and good examples occur south of Duznau (5376), and north-west and east of Siggenreute (5376). The long axes of these drumlins lie from south-west to north-east, and the hills are blunt to the south-west and taper to the north-east. This is repeated in most of the drumlins of the eastern half of the area. As drumlins are generally elongated in the direction of ice movement, with their tapering ends facing downstream, this indicates a probable north-easterly spread of the ice in this part of the great glacier lobe. It should be noted that the shape of these hills has been emphasized on the map by the addition of form-lines between the contours. The normal contour interval is 10 m, but in some instances form-lines of 2·5 m, 5 m, and 7·5 m have been interpolated between them. In the west of our area the shape of the hills is less regular, and the direction of their long axes suggests a more northerly movement of the ice.

The irregular hollows between the drumlins may form enclosed basins containing lakes. Generally, however, they are filled with patches of bog (Manzenmoos, 5476) or covered with wet pastures. Some of the latter are drained by man-made water channels, and though in many areas the lakes are used as fishponds (*Weiher*), here these are the parallel channels of the Hermannsberger Weiher (5275, 5276) and the single water-channel of the Langmoosweiher (5277). It is obvious that, in a country of irregularly dumped deposits, drainage is poorly integrated, and in some of the small streams the direction of flow (shown by arrows) is confusing. Artificial water-channels are numerous, and some link up natural streams, and in so doing cross low watersheds. It is interesting to follow the water-channels from Langmoosweiher to the small lakes or reservoirs (marked in blue) north of Esseratsweiler (5375, 5475), and to note the watersheds and the flow of the streams.

The river Argen crosses the area in the north, entering it from the north-east. It has cut a valley about 50 m deep in the boulder clay and gravels (note the three gravel pits, 5075, 5076), and the outer curves of its meanders are undercutting the valley walls, forming steep slopes which in places reach over 70 m. Near Steinenbach there is a considerable widening of the valley floor, and indications of long-abandoned meanders which formerly made embayments in the northern valley side. Although four hamlets and the outskirts of a fifth are shown in the valley, it is curiously cut off from the rest of the region, and only one bridge is marked which is capable of carrying even country-lane traffic. This may be due to the fact that the river is here a rural district boundary for two-thirds of its length, and that Achberg, as stated on the map, is an isolated

Landesvermessungsamt Baden-Württemberg

Topographische Karte 1/25 000

Extract from SHEET 8324

WANGEN-WEST

part of the rural district of Sigmaringen, far away in the Swabian Alb. Beyond our region the river finally swings south to flow into Lake Constance. The map margin of the full sheet tells us that the adjoining rural district to the south is that of Lindau, which is a small Bavarian town on the northern shore of Lake Constance, and the lake is actually less than 8 km (5 miles) distant. (The state boundary, which in three places in the south just enters the mapped area, is that which separates Baden-Württemberg from Bavaria.)

The agricultural landscape of this region, with its repetition of hummocks and hollows, appears as a pattern of woodlands and pastures, arable strips, and fruit-gardens. Its land use is varied, and the many forester's paths in the woodlands, the drainage ditches in the wetter lowlands, the embanked, and in some places terraced, fields, and the carefully routed and built country roads all suggest good husbandry and careful preservation. At first sight the forests and pastures would seem the dominating vegetation cover, and coniferous woodland almost completely clothes some of the eastern drumlins, while the mixed Schloss forestlands extend over most of the slopes south of the Argen. In the west tree cover is less extensive, though the Dickenen (5077 and neighbouring squares) and Meerholz have larger woodlands. Apart from marshy patches, a very large part of the morainic floor is pasture, but though it is mainly confined to the lowlands in the east, in the west it covers many drumlin slopes and in some cases reaches to the summits. But arable land is also widespread. Many of the western drumlins are largely under cultivation, and fields have replaced parts of the lowland pastures. In Achberg the arable areas are smaller, but there are many rectangular patches and strips on the hillsides. Achberg has most of the hop-gardens, and though these vary greatly in size, they are found on the hillsides in the neighbourhood of every settlement within the district. Orchards, too, abound throughout the whole mapped area, often planted in hillside pastures, and everywhere present in the gardens which surround the hamlets. Spreading north from Lake Constance, the vine appears in one district only—Rengersweiler, in the extreme south-west—and the vineyards have climbed to over 500 m on its sunny southern slopes.

The population is gathered into many small and loosely knit settlements sited between the drumlins, and some of them consist of only a few buildings in the midst of orchards and gardens. Single houses are rare, though there is some dispersal in the south. The map marks two sawmills and one brick-kiln, but otherwise agriculture is the only activity of the region. Esseratsweiler appears to be a small community centre with a web of radiating roads, for although no main road enters the region, there is a very close net of narrower country roads. These pass from one drumlin to another, curving round their bases, even cutting into their slopes with the support of embankments on the valley sides. Where intervening marshy hollows must be crossed the roads are carried on the summit of embankments. The few miles of road linking Esseratsweiler–Duznau–Siberatsweiler–Gunderatsweiler reflect clearly the characteristics of drumlin relief.

Maps for Further Study
Topographische Karte 1/50 000   Sheet L 8324   Wangen im Allgäu
The more extensive region covered by this map gives a good general picture of morainic country. Not all the area is drumlin-covered, but it is a land of irregular dumps; marshes and forest patches abound, and there are many lakes. The rivers meander south-westward in incised valleys.
Geologische Übersichtskarte von Baden-Württemberg 1/200 000   Sheet 4   Third Edition 1962
This excellent map is expensive, but it covers an area stretching from Lake Constance to the Swabian Alb. It includes the great fans of moraine left by the ice lobes of the Riss and Würm glaciers, which spread northward from the Alps beyond Lake Constance. Riss and Würm moraines are differentiated, and drumlins and recessional and terminal moraines are shown.

Limestone Landscape: The Swabian Alb near Urach

Landesvermessungsamt Baden-Württemberg. Topographische Karte 1/50 000
L 7522 URACH

The Swabian Alb (or Jura) forms part of a high cuesta of Jurassic limestones, which continue the folded limestones of the Jura mountains. In the Klettgau, near the Swiss frontier, the Alb forms a narrow belt, but as it sweeps north-eastward through Württemberg it greatly increases in width, reaching 45–50 km. In Bavaria it swings northward as the Franconian Alb.

The Swabian plateau is high, reaching well over 1000 m in the south-west, but gradually decreasing in height eastward. Its surface is built of massive limestones of the Upper Jurassic, and their light-coloured cliffs crown the summits of the scarp. The steep scarp slopes face north-westward, and overlook the valleys of the Neckar and its tributaries, while the dip slopes descend very gently to the south-east, finally to disappear under Tertiary sediments or a cover of moraine. Underlying the limestones are the much less resistant beds of the Middle Jurassic, and these form the foothill country to the north of the scarp.

THE MAP-SHEET
Note. It is important that the full map-sheet *1/50 000 L7522 Urach* should be available for study. However, place-names in the text which are printed in heavy type occur in the map-extract.

The area covered by the selected map-sheet lies in the northern Alb, and comprises a small area of the foothills, a short length of the dissected scarp, and a part of the main plateau. The foothills lie in the north and and west, form a gently dissected country, abundantly watered, with a host of small streams which join the larger rivers flowing from the valleys and embayments of the Alb—the Steinach from the **Neuffen embayment**, the Lauter from the **Oberlenningen valley**, the Lindach from the Neidlingen embayment. Everywhere orchards cover the slopes, and there are vineyards on a few favoured hillsides, while farther north mixed woodlands spread over low spurs. Isolated farms are very rare, but large villages and small towns are strung out along the rivers, and follow each other at only a few kilometres distance along the foot of the slopes below the main scarp. In some settlements a clearly defined compact nucleus suggests a medieval origin as a small walled town. **Neuffen** and Owen are two examples of this, each over-looked by a ruined castle spectacularly perched on limestone crags, and probably once the home of the town's overlord. Many settlements have some industrial development. (Paper-mills, brick-works and saw-mills were named in earlier editions of this map, and other factories—often light metal or textile works—were marked but their nature not disclosed.) Besides its vineyards (the centre of its life for centuries and still producing a highly prized wine), Neuffen has modern industrial development in the exploitation of a vast limestone quarry, two kilometres to the south, to which it is connected by cable or suspension railway.

The main scarp of the Alb is very steep and rises over 200 m like a great cliff. When seen from the distance, in an approach from the north, it appears as a long, unbroken front, but the map shows that for a depth of many kilometres long, narrow valleys have almost separated large and small plateau areas from the main Alb. Some of these have been still further reduced to narrow, sinuous ridges, 'peninsulas' of highland (*e.g.* the Hörnle or headland south of Neuffen, and of Teck east of Owen). Some areas have been completely isolated, and form flat-topped or even conical residual hills. Our sheet covers a short length of this dissected border. The Lauter valley penetrates the plateau for 6 km, and two of its headstreams have cut lateral valleys parallel to the plateau front. The **valley of the Erms**, in the west, penetrates far deeper into the Alb, extending another 6 km to the south of **Urach**, where the gorge of a lateral tributary continues the dissection eastward. From Urach, **the Elsach tributary** can be traced upstream to its source below the **Falkensteiner Cave**, which is separated by a neck of plateau, hardly a kilometre in width, from the gorge of the Lauter tributary. Here dissection has gone far towards isolating from the main Alb the whole plateau area shown in our map-extract. The process is carried still

further in the plateau north of the Fils valley, which is included in the north-east of the whole map-sheet area. The labyrinth of valleys has nearly completed the subdivision of this plateau strip, and the autobahn, passing through Gruibingen, follows a valley which has opened a relatively easy passage to the lowlands north of the scarp, so providing a shortened route from Stuttgart across the Alb to Ulm, and so to Munich.

Both on the Alb front and in the valleys, the scarp slopes are covered with a band of deciduous forest and crowned with limestone crags or *felsen*. These occur everywhere, and particularly good examples are seen on the **summits east of Hochwang overlooking Oberlenningen.** The scarp forests are a most conspicuous landscape feature. In places they spread over the adjacent plateau surface, but often they end abruptly at the summit, and their lower boundary is remarkably level for long stretches, bordering the orchards in an even line. At the base of the main scarp is a most important spring-line. (This marks the junction of the Upper Jurassic limestones and the less permeable beds of the Middle Jurassic. It is the erosion of these softer beds which has brought about the dissection of the Alb and the recession of its front.)

The lower and broader sections of the valleys share the characteristics of the lands north of the Alb front, but their upper sections rapidly narrow and become wooded ravines. Though in some cases very steep, they provide the easiest ascents to the plateau, and roads attempting to climb the scarp do so only by means of tremendous hairpin bends. A number of settlements lie in the main valleys, and they differ greatly in plan. Some, like Urach and the smaller Wiesensteig, which are far up their valleys and partly enclosed by wooded slopes, are compact. Others, like Oberlenningen and Dettingen, which are nearer the Alb front, are much more open in plan, and large parts of them appear modern developments. The plan of **Urach** strongly suggests that it originated as a medieval walled town, with a central market-place and radiating streets, and the castle of **Hohenurach** overlooking the town from a headland of the western scarp. From the massed buildings of its nucleus, sited between the Erms and the Elsach, it has spread up the valleys which converge upon it, and down the wider valley of the Erms. Urach must have enjoyed the status of a town for a very long period, and throughout its history has probably had many administrative functions. Industry is clearly established in these valleys, and spinning-mills, paper-mills, and paper and bleaching works (and formerly saw-mills) are individually marked, but there are many factories whose work has not been specified. The enormous **works of Oberlenningen** (paper-works) must draw hundreds of workers from both valley and plateau, and **Hochwang** has the appearance of a small housing-estate specially served by a skilfully engineered road, which does not appear on the map published in 1949. Branch railway-lines serve all the three river valleys—Erms, Lauter, and Fils—and Urach, Oberlenningen, and Wiesensteig are railway terminals.

In sharp contrast to the wooded valleys, and 250 m–300 m above them, stretch the great landscapes of the plateau. But this is not the barren and harsh country that one might expect in an area of massive limestone. **The plateau area of the map-extract** has large and gentle undulations, with low rounded summits covered with mixed forest, or, less frequently, wholly coniferous forest. There are no poverty-stricken areas with rock exposures; instead tree-lined roads cross an agricultural land, and link large villages surrounded with gardens. Extensive patches of pasture are indicated, but this does not necessarily mean open grazing-ground, as here cattle are stall-fed, and hay and other fodder is cut daily and carried green to the cattle-sheds. The map does not distinguish unfenced roads, nor can it reveal that the fields are also unhedged strips, often curving with the contours. But it does show that the lower boundaries of some woodlands outline the slopes, and that ridges between fields often do the same (3075, and on the whole sheet 4579, and the district around Westerheim and Feldstetten). Together these features build a characteristic, wide and uncluttered landscape.

The full sheet shows that farther south changes occur. There are more numerous and higher summits, larger areas of carefully preserved forests, and much greater expanses of rough pasture, dotted with bushes, and broken by rock exposures and patches of stony waste-land. The villages are more widely separated, very compact, and sited in hollows. But they are ringed with gardens, and, as indicated by the network of field paths, surrounded by cultivated land. Good roads join them, more often than not tree-lined. The trees may be useful guides in winter, when a blanket of snow covers the Alb for many weeks. (Three ski-chalets and a ski-jump are shown on the map.)

It is perhaps not surprising that in this open and rather empty land there should be an army

training centre, with large barracks close to Münsingen. This is by far the largest plateau
settlement shown, and has the appearance of an old town. The rectangular plan of its compact
nucleus suggests that it was once walled, and the narrow roads that enclose this nucleus would
appear to mark the former site of these walls. Münsingen is the administrative centre for a very
large area, as the administrative boundaries show, and the name 'Münsinger Alb' suggests. It
is naturally the focus of many routes across the Alb, and is served by one of the few plateau
railways.

But though the plateau does not have a strikingly barren appearance, karstic features abound.
The most fundamental is the lack of surface water—the plateau has no streams. In the whole
of the plateau area east of Münsingen there is not one natural stream. There is, however, much
underground water. All the deeply incised valleys which dissect the northern front have strongly
flowing rivers, and a host of small tributaries join them from the springs of the plateau sides.
(These springs issue at the junction of the Middle and the Upper Jurassic rocks, but some issue
higher up the scarp within the Upper Jurassic, and fall over the escarpment below as waterfalls.)
But even these deep valleys, when traced upward to the plateau, have a head stretch which has
only intermittent water-flow or is completely dry. There are numerous examples, such as the
valley south of Schlattstall (3675), the Hasental above the source of the Fils (4478), Brucktal
with intermittent water-flow (3671), and a dry valley-head leading up to Zainingen. **In the area
of the map-extract**, **Mauchental** and **Kaltental**, respectively south and east of **Hülben**, are
other examples. The intermittent streams flow when the water-table is especially high—after
a long period of rain, for example, or when snows melt in the spring.

A large number of reservoirs and wells are shown, at least one reservoir for each settlement.
Zainingen retains its large central cistern or pond, but it is likely that, along with all the other
plateau villages, it now has a piped water-supply. The Randecker Maar (3682), a well-watered
hollow in the limestones, introduces another feature which only a geological map can show in
detail. *Maar* means crater, and in the **Urach district** a very large number of volcanic necks
occur. Many of these are found on the plateau, and are filled with basalt tuff and breccia, and
two-thirds of the villages in the mapped area are sited on these necks. The choice of these necks
as sites in nearly every possible case shows clearly that this has definite advantages—perhaps
a better water-supply, perhaps richer and deeper soil.

In the south-east of the plateau a river does flow on the surface, and is of great interest. Just
south of Sirchingen (2968) a wide and open dry valley is shown, which curves through Lonsingen
to Gächingen. Here the Gächinger Lauter flows intermittently in the valley, but lower down it
becomes permanent, and at Gomadingen joins the Great Lauter. This river is a tributary of the
Danube, and in a long, gentle descent (very different from those of the northern valleys) it flows
southward across the dip slope of the Alb. This means that Sirchingen marks part of the watershed
between the Neckar and the Danube river systems, yet Sirchingen is only a kilometre from the
northward-flowing Erms. Münsingen also lies south of this watershed. Its valley, the Baumtal,
has been linked to the town by an artificial water-channel, and below this appears dry. Three
other dry valleys of the plateau dip slope are the wooded Muhltal west of Magolsheim (4363),
the Rummeltal east of the same village, and the Eistal, which extends from south of Enderlesberg
(4366) to the eastern limit of the mapped area (4864).

The plateau surface has other karstic features. In the rather confused relief of hummocks and
hollows there are many completely enclosed depressions of various sizes, even some over a
kilometre across. These are shown by depression contours, and are distinguished by arrows
showing the slope of descent. They are widespread, and good examples occur east of Ennabeuren
(4867), north of Hengen (3472), and south of **Erkenbrechtsweiler** (3179) in the map-extract.
Besides these large depressions great numbers of swallow-holes (*Dolinen*) are marked. These sinks
—so typical of limestone areas—are scattered singly or in groups. In only three of them is any
surface water shown to disappear. A peat-pit (3880) lies in a hollow to the north of Schopfloch,
and it is bordered on the east and west by small enclosed depressions. Each of these contains a
swallow-hole, and water drains into these from the peat, forming in one case a waterfall. The
presence of the peat is explained only by the geological map, which shows in this area a small
patch of Tertiary clay overlying the limestone. The waters of two small springs also disappear
into a swallow-hole just east of Donnstetten (4275). Examples of dry dolines are shown near the
Sturrenbühl (4663), and, in the map-extract, on the pastures north of **Grabenstetten** and in

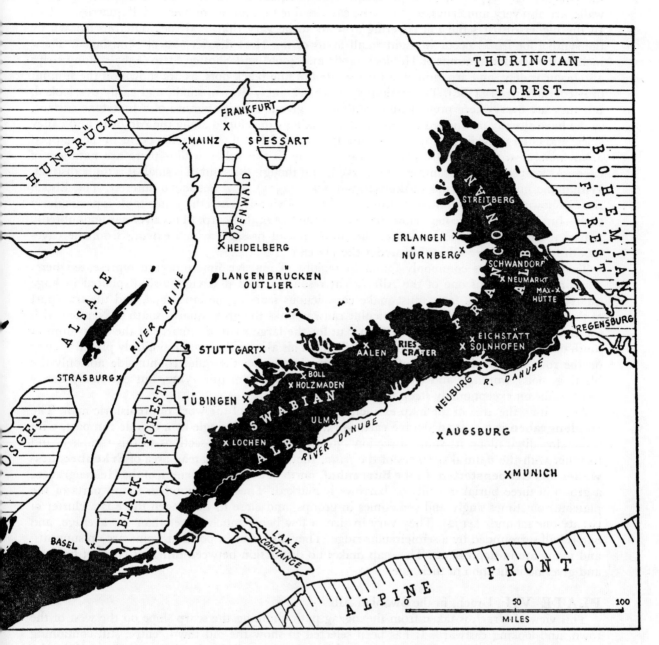

FIG. 5. JURASSIC OUTCROPS OF THE SWABIAN AND FRANCONIAN JURA

Reproduced by permission of the publishers, Messrs Oliver and Boyd, from W. J. Arkell's "Jurassic Geology of the World"

The Jurassic rocks represented in Dr Arkell's map include the whole Jurassic series—softer Liassic rocks (Lower Jurassic) as well as the sandstones, limestone-bands, and clays of the Middle Jurassic, and the harder Upper Jurassic limestones of the Alb. Aalen lies in the Middle Jurassic outcrops, as does the north-western area represented in the Urach map-sheet, but Boll and Holzmaden are situated in the Liassic areas, well north of the dissected Alb scarp.

the village itself (3476). Small depressions, without sinks and incompletely surrounded by steep walls, are also very numerous, and may be cavities due to solution, or even small quarries (4763). In the higher districts the soil covering appears to be very thin, and rock outcrops (shown by the symbol for *felsen*) occur in eight small areas of the Hart district east of Münsingen. These include the wooded summits of Höhloch (4065 and 4066) and Shotten Stein (4367). Stony strips also occur widely, and are indicated by a symbol of fine black dots, as are shown on the summit of Niederhöklingen (4568). The various symbols are finely drawn, small, and easily overlooked, but they are everywhere present and combine to give a definite picture of a limestone surface.

We have already mentioned the cliffs, most strikingly developed along the Alb front and valley sides, and often providing impregnable sites for castles. Nine of these castles occur in the mapped area, some most dramatically placed. Also—chiefly in the valley walls—there are numbers of caves. At least seventeen examples are marked, and though the symbol is small it is quite distinct. Within the map-extract, the **Falkensteiner Cave**(3375) is of particular interest. The Elsach river is shown to flow intermittently from this cave—obviously when the water-table is particularly high—but its usual source lies below the cave, at the foot of the scarp. (This river has undoubtedly played a large part in the erosion of the subterranean passage, which extends from the cave-mouth for nearly three kilometres under the plateau.)

Two other features commonly found in regions of massive limestone are represented here. The limestone itself is one of the Alb's great resources, and it is vigorously exploited in huge quarries. The raw rock faces must make conspicuous scars in the landscape, and the transport of the stone presents problems. A funicular railway links the great quarry south of Neuffen with the railway station north of the old town, but for the large roadside quarry at the scarp summit south of **Hülben** only road transport is available. This also applies to the similarly placed quarry on the road from Hülben to Neuffen. This must impose on the quiet countryside not only the blasting, noisy working, and clouds of dust inseparable from quarrying, but extremely heavy lorry traffic on exceptionally steep roads.

Also within the area of the map-extract, there is evidence of the work of prehistoric man. The **Heidengraben** is a great defensive earthwork, and is either a single or a double rampart, with a flanking ditch along its western section (3077). There are four sections to this rampart, and together with the natural defences of the *felsen*, they enclose the plateau area of **Erkenbrechts-weiler** and **Grabenstetten**. In the **Bürrenhof**, north of the western length of the Heidengraben, a group of three burial mounds or barrows is marked. These are found in many parts of the plateau, sometimes singly and sometimes in groups, and close to Zainingen there is a cluster of twenty-one mounds (4172). They vary in size, a few being much larger than the average, and one is half surrounded by a semicircular ridge. They also vary in position: some are on summits, and many are in depressions. The map makes no distinction between different types of barrows and gives no indication of their age.

PLATE VII   Urach, in the Swabian Alb

This view of Urach is taken from the zigzag path climbing the scarp slope on the west of the town, and looking eastward. It has been selected to show the old town centre, still containing many old gabled buildings, and a reminder of its former walls in the ring road that half circles it on the south and east. A number of big industrial concerns are housed in clean modern factories, bordering the Elsach, on the north side of the town, and on the left side of the picture. There are many other factory buildings farther down the valley, but outside the photograph. These are not necessarily new developments. Urach built her first paper-mill in 1477, and her textile industries have been very long established. The modern growth of the town is clearly seen in the new houses climbing the hillsides, and spreading up the valleys which cut into the Alb—the Pfaler Tal (Elsach Valley) opposite the viewer, the Mauchental to the left, and the entrance to the upper Erms valley to the right. Above the scarps and their woodlands (in which many clearings have been made) the level surface of the plateau can be seen. The houses of Graben-stetten are just visible, with low wooded heights behind them on the horizon.

Maps for Further Study

1. *1/25 000 Umgebungskarte Urach*

This map—in which Urach is centrally placed—is built up of parts of four regular 1/25 000

PLATE VII. Urach, in the Swabian Alb

Photo: Robert Holder, Urach

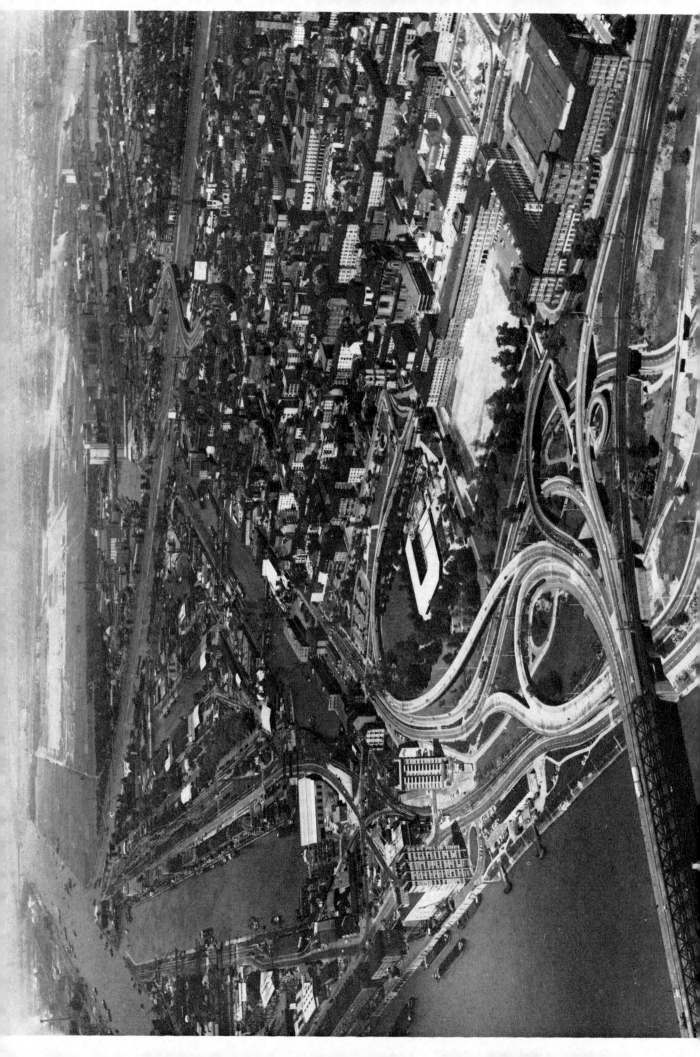

sheets. Note (i) the medieval plan of central Neuffen and Urach, (ii) the vineyards east of Neuffen, west of Kohlberg, and around the Hofbühl and Florianberg north of Neuhausen, (iii) the quarries and factories.

2. *Geologische Übersichtskarte von Baden-Württemberg 1/200 000 Sheet 4*
It has already been suggested that this map be used for the study of the moraines north of Lake Constance. It also covers part of the Alb, and includes Urach and Münsingen, besides illustrating well some of the dry and intermittent stream valleys of the plateau, and the many old volcanic necks in the Urach area, which are filled with basalt tuff. The Alb scarp is not included, but is shown in Sheets 2 and 3 in the same map series.

Illustrations
Two attractive and useful collections of photographs are: *Urach und seine Alb*, Robert Holder Verlag, Urach, Württemberg. *Die Schwäbische Alb*, Jan Thorbecke Verlag, Konstanz, Württemberg.

Rhine Rift-valley: Urban Landscape of Mannheim and Ludwigshafen

Landesvermessungsamt Baden-Württemberg. Topographische Karte 1/50 000
L 6516 MANNHEIM

The cities of Mannheim and Ludwigshafen lie in the lower rift-valley of the Rhine, and front each other across the river at the point where it receives the tributary Neckar. Mannheim, in Baden-Württemberg, lies south of the Neckar, and was formerly confined between it and the Rhine, but has now straddled across this tributary to its northern bank. Ludwigshafen, stretching along the left bank of the Rhine, lies in the Rhineland-Palatinate. Baden-Württemberg and the Rhineland-Palatinate are two of the eleven states (or *Länder*) that compose the Federal Republic of West Germany, and so the Rhine, separating these two cities, is also here a state boundary.
This section of the rift-valley is about thirty-seven kilometres in width, and is bordered by the Odenwald Mountains on the east and by the Hardt Mountains on the west. The Odenwald, rising to over five hundred metres, and bounded on the west by faults, border the valley in a long wall, but the Hardt, rather higher and also bounded on the valley side by faults, form a less regular margin. The valley floor lies about 100 metres above sea-level and is mainly filled with terraces of Quaternary sand and gravels, with large areas covered by loess on the western side, while on the eastern side the Neckar has deposited a great spread of river gravels and alluvium (Fig. 6). Similar sediments line the courses of many other streams where they leave their deeply incised valleys in the mountains and enter the rift-valley. Between the western loess country and the Rhine, a low intermediate terrace of river gravels stretches in a wide arc from Speyer to Worms. This terrace lies only a few metres above the Rhine flood-plain, but on its western margin there is a sharp rise to the higher loess country.

The Rhine flood-plain lies a little to the east of the centre of the rift-valley, and is about twelve kilometres wide at Mannheim and six to seven kilometres above Altrip. Within it the Rhine sweeps in great meanders. A swift and powerful river, carrying tremendous floods in early summer, it has been controlled by embanking and realignment. The cut-off loops remain as ox-bow lakes or as marshy tracts, and with the remnants of generations of former meanders—which have been abandoned by downstream migration or the natural shifting of the river-course—they form a complicated maze of water-channels. The present flood-plain lies a few metres below the sand and gravel terraces, and the margin of these has been cut by the outer curves of the meanders into a scalloped edge.
The pattern of land utilization and settlement is closely allied to these various features. The mountains are green with forests to their summits, except that on both sides of the valley vine-

PLATE VIII *(opposite)*.   Mannheim's Docklands   *Photo Mannheim Tourist Office*

yards cover the lower slopes. A line of settlements is strung along the foot of the castle-crowned spurs of the Hardt. Most of these are engaged in viticulture, and the district is famous for its wines, while some of the towns have long-established textile and other industries. A similar line of old villages and small towns occurs at the foot of the Odenwald. The river deposits brought down by the Neckar and other streams from the highland rim are cultivated, but in some places the dyking of the streams, the patches of marsh, and the ditches in the fields indicate waterlogging, and the need for careful drainage and protection from floods. The low terraces built of the Quaternary sands and gravels, and reaching altitudes of 110 metres, are much drier, and are largely forested. East of the Rhine many of these sandy areas are empty of settlement, though some large villages are found on their margins, where many springs may occur. In the west, where loess has cloaked these deposits and the terraces are higher, the land is very fertile and well-cultivated, and the vine extends from the lower slopes of the mountains and spreads far into the rift-valley. Here villages are specially numerous on the banks of the many streams that cross the area from the Hardt, and also along the well-defined margin of these lands to the east. The much lower arc of gravel terrace edging the Rhine flood-plain is poorer, but a number of settlements are found on the bluffs overlooking the river. The Rhine flood-plain itself presents a landscape of many lakes, loops of marsh and peat in abandoned meanders, and thickets of bushes and trees around many of its water-courses. However, there are some isolated dyked pastures, and even a few patches of ditched and cultivated land. On the whole, settlement has avoided the flood-plain in the past, owing to the ravages of the river. Now the huge conurbation of Mannheim-Ludwigshafen has not only attracted a great population to the banks of the Rhine but daily draws a vast army of workers from scores of villages and towns in the rift-valley and beyond.

THE MAP-SHEET

In this sheet the towns of Mannheim and Ludwigshafen are almost centrally placed, so that their relationship to the immediate neighbourhood is excellently shown. However, the area covered by the map-sheet does not include the whole width of the rift-valley, but only extends far enough east to reach the lowest fringe of the Odenwald slopes, and westward does not even reach to the loess-covered terraces. The dominating physical features shown are short stretches of the Rhine and Neckar, and that these were formerly wild and erratic rivers, with shifting courses, is clearly indicated by the number of abandoned river-channels. These are not the meanders of old age but the work of powerful rivers, subject to violent floods, and burdened with great quantities of detritus. Only about twenty-four kilometres of the Rhine flood-plain are shown on the map-sheet, but in that distance there are the clearly marked traces of at least ten abandoned meanders, apart from the **Altrhein at Waldhof**, which has been cut off by man. Some of these appear to show down-stream displacement (*e.g.*, those to the south of Altrip), and many have bitten deeply into the river gravels and sands of the terrace to the west of our area. The low bluffs of 3–5 metres which surround the embayments and form peninsulas between them are the sites of many settlements—Altrip, Neuhofen, Rheingonheim, Maudach, Mundenheim, Oggersheim, Friesenheim, Frankenthal, Roxheim, and Bobenheim, and, in a similar position to the east of the river, Lampertheim. The Neckar, too, has wandered widely over its fan of detritus, and remains of former channels are shown even beyond Lützelsachsen.

As cut-offs of all ages are clearly shown, examples of every stage in their infilling and near-obliteration can be studied. In some cases, where all lakes, bogs, and marshes have disappeared the tracks of field paths or old roads may still recall their form.

But the Neckar and Rhine are now controlled, and disastrous changes of course cannot occur. The Neckar is embanked, and from the short length of its course shown here it is clear that the river has been canalized. In two stretches—from above Ilvesheim to below **Neuostheim**, and from the bridge above Eppelheim to Schwabenheim—a second channel north of the river has been cut. Each of these is closed by locks at its down-stream end, before its re-entry into the river. Weirs at Wieblingen and above Ilvesheim control the flow of water into these canal channels.

The Rhine enters our region as a wide and strong, but nevertheless subdued, river, as tremendous undertakings of realignment and water-control have been completed up-stream. In the stretch shown, an important realigned channel is the straight **Friesenheim cutting below Ludwigshafen**, which has formed Friesenheim Island and left the old channel as a great dock

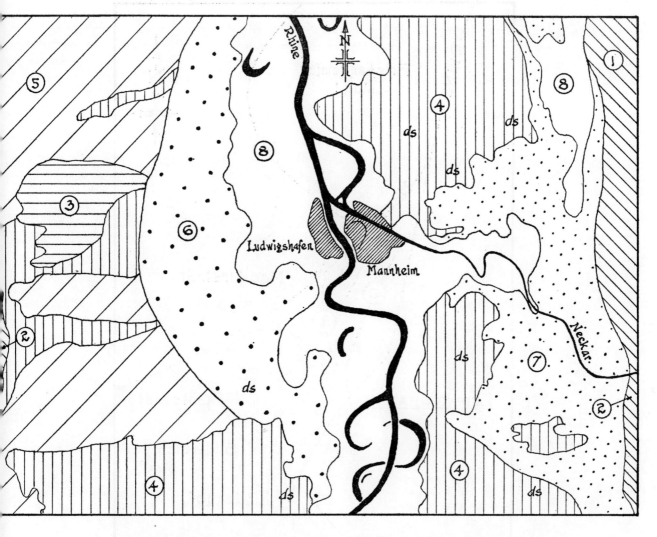

FIG. 6. MUCH SIMPLIFIED GEOLOGICAL SKETCH-MAP OF THE RHINE RIFT
VALLEY IN THE REGION OF MANNHEIM-LUDWIGSHAFEN

Based on the Geologische Übersichtskarte von Baden-Württemberg 1/200 000, by permission of the Geological Survey of Baden-Württemberg

1. } Crystalline rocks (1) and Bunter Sandstone (2) of the rift-valley walls.
2. }

3. Mainly Tertiary (Pliocene) sands and gravels.
4. Mainly Quaternary (Middle and Upper Pleistocene) sands and gravels.
5. Loess and loam.
6. Mainly coarse river debris and sands.
7. Finer river deposits of the Neckar fan.
8. Alluvium of present flood-plains.
ds. Dunes.

Note. The numerous river tributaries crossing the higher western terraces have cut the deposits here into strips, and the distribution of these is more elaborate than shown in the simplified sketch-map.

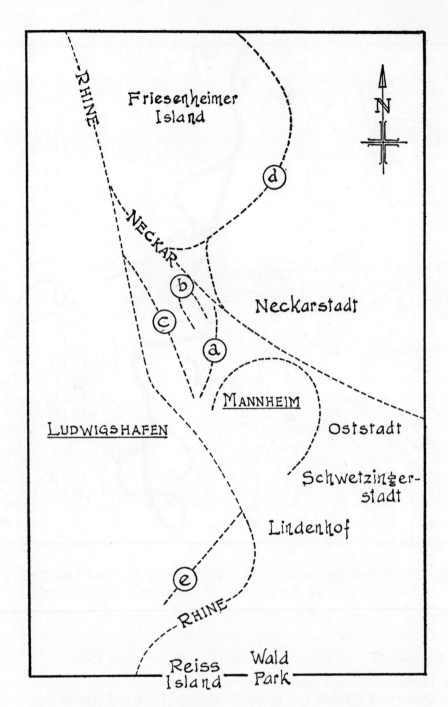

FIG. 7. DISTRICTS OF MANNHEIM AND RHINE HARBOURS
SCALE 1/50 000

a. Verbindungs Canal.
b. Inner Harbour (two basins).
c. Mühlau Harbour.
d. Industry Harbour.
e. Luitpold Harbour.

All harbours east of the Rhine are part of the Port of Mannheim.

basin for Mannheim. The river is embanked, but a multitude of dykes some distance back are an additional protection to the river flats. However, drifting ice, particularly in the Neckar, and great flood-waters in both the Rhine and the Neckar occur from time to time, and in spite of all protective installations put many dock buildings, railways, and roads temporarily out of action.

West of the Rhine only a fringe of the low terrace is included in the map, and this is seen to be agricultural, but east of the Rhine two areas of forested terrace are shown. The nature of these is indicated by the complete absence of all water-courses, and by such names as Sandhofen and Sandtorf (both west of the northern forest) and Sandgrube (west of the southern forest). But if surface water is wanting, abundant springs are found at Lampertheim, and especially at Viernheim on the margins of the northern terrace. A series of long, narrow ridges, rising to 110 metres, crosses this area from north to south, dividing it into two sections, while a second series of ridges borders it on the east. In the west the trees are mainly conifers, and the central area is a wooded heathland rather than a forest. In the east an increasing number of deciduous trees appear.

Three-quarters of this whole extensive area lies in Hesse, and here the forests are state-owned, with a close and regular system of forest rides. As the map shows, this is reserved as a hunting-ground, with a resident game-warden and shooting-butts. A much smaller area of the forest lies in Baden-Württemberg, and along its southern borders residential building, especially in the neighbourhood of Käfertal and the Garden City, has made encroachments. Mannheim is only about five kilometres distant, and the woodlands lie within its urban boundaries. It is obvious that the city recognizes their recreational value, and at least part of them is open to the public (note the roads and paths, the nature reservation, the bar, and the siting of the Children's Convalescent Home—Kindererholungsheim).

The southern forest between the Neckar and the Rhine has also been encroached upon by the industrial development of Rheinau, by great electrical works, and by Mannheim's enormous marshalling yards.

Between the Viernheim forests and the Odenwald mountains lie the waterlogged flats of the closely embanked Old and New Weschnitz rivers and other small streams from the hills. The lands around them are wet pastures intersected by a maze of drainage ditches, but a scattering of trees marks the drier agricultural land extending to the Odenwald. These types of country spread into the great fan of the Neckar, where old meanders are clearly marked between Heddesheim and Lützelsachsen. The confused drainage of this pasture-land, and the ditched streams from the Hohensachsen, finally drain away northward to join the Weschnitz waters, and ultimately the Rhine. The rest of the fan included within the map boundaries is both higher and drier. The Kanzelbach and the Rohmbach from the Odenwald both reach the Neckar, but some waters of the former sink into the ground, and all hill streams between Schriesheim and Grossachsen do likewise. The spring of Galgbrunnen rises in the flood-plain of the Neckar, and not in the fan itself, which has no marked springs, and appears to be porous. It is everywhere cultivated, and symbols are so carefully mapped that the features of the rural landscape (such as the rows of trees lining the field paths) are immediately apparent. But no map can reveal the bright, coloured mosaic of the hedgeless field-strips, with their rich variety of crops.

However, although the map-sheet contains much information about the Rhine, and illustrates many of the characteristic deposits of the rift-valley floor, it has also been selected for its representation of the industrial and **urban landscape of Mannheim-Ludwigshafen**, and this has been included in the chosen extract. (See Fig. 7.)

The most striking feature of Mannheim is the grid-plan of its central area, and the broad boulevard which encloses this in a great horseshoe with an inner, narrower ring-road clearly discernible. Both these and the eleven N.E.–S.W. parallel roads of the central grid are planned in relation to **the Schloss**, which overlooks the river Rhine on a slightly raised bluff. In many old towns broad boulevards enclosing a compact central core of buildings outline the site of former fortifications, and old town plans of Mannheim show this to be the case here.

Enclosed within the Neckar and the Rhine, and bounded on the west by the Verbindungs Canal, modern Mannheim could expand freely and uninterruptedly only to the east. However, across the Neckar, on its northern bank, has grown up a compact suburb (Neckarstadt) to which it is linked by three bridges. The plan of this and the new suburbs to the east has been related to older Mannheim in such a manner that the city appears as a coherent whole. Oststadt is related to a broad boulevard, which is a continuation of the main street of the old city (the Planken), and in its basic rectilinear design it is in keeping with older Mannheim. It is clear that this suburb, with its fine main road (the entry of the autobahn from Heidelberg into the city), its public and private gardens, and its open and spacious building, is a civic area of distinction. To the north of it lies the green belt of Luisen Park, and to the south the closely built Schwetzingen Stadt. Though this is less obviously planned in relation to the old town, many of its streets are continuous with those of the grid, or with those of Oststadt, and with them it makes an integrated whole. Neckarstadt, although it is cut off from the parent city by the Neckar, does not appear isolated, as its main streets radiate from a bridge-head which is a continuation of the central road in the ancient grid. Lindenhof, however, is separated more completely from the rest of the city by enormous marshalling yards. Though backed by industrial works as well as these yards, it is situated adjoining the river, and with large private gardens and a strip of park along the Rhine it appears to be at least partly residential. It is fortunate for Mannheim that for over eight kilometres (five miles) the river-front is open and beautiful. The Schloss gardens and the tree-lined Rhine promenade bordering southern Lindenhof lead, without any interruption of industrial or commercial building, to the extensive Waldpark and its Nature Sanctuary of Rheiss Island and the river beaches beyond. This water-front and the gracious approach to the city from the east, whether they be due to fortuitous circumstance or to wise planning, are great assets. But nevertheless Mannheim is now above everything else an important river port and industrial centre. The triangular flats to the north-west of the city are the site of its great commercial docks, and the map shows three dock basins. The Verbindungs Canal (formerly an abandoned arm of the Rhine) adjoins the city, and connects by gates with the Neckar. The Mühlau basin opens directly from the Rhine and is over two kilometres (1½ miles) long, and the inner docks, with two basins, open like the Verbindungs Canal into the Neckar. All these docks and the Rhine water-front are lined with quays and dock installations. The map shows the lines of long buildings—certainly warehouses—and the multitude of railway tracks on the quays. If there is one disadvantage of the site it would appear to be the narrowness of the link with the marshalling yards south-east of Mannheim. The miles of dock quays, the warehousing facilities, and the size of the marshalling yards are a clear indication of the enormous amount of goods transhipped and distributed from this region. Across the Neckar, along the banks of the Friesenheimer Altrhein, factories and industrial works follow each other for miles. Uncramped, with a long water-front and good rail connections, this is a great industrial port, the Industriehafen. It is interesting to compare the dock landscape of this area with that of the commercial basins west of Mannheim, and to note its unhampered spread of buildings, the large number of factory chimneys, and the disposition of the railway tracks. Industrial development has also spread inland, to Käfertal, north-east of Mannheim, and to Friedrichsfeld, to the south-east. Another port has been built at Rheinau, seven kilometres south of Mannheim, with four large basins excavated in the flood-plain, and an important quay at Neckarau. A long line of works and factories has been built on the edge of the terrace, linking Rheinau and Neckarau, and still there is room for development. Here, then, around these waterways and away from the city, is concentrated most of the commercial and industrial activity of Mannheim.

The urban landscape of Ludwigshafen is completely different from that of Mannheim. The town has spread north and south along the Rhine, and north-westward and south-westward, linking up with Friesenheim and Mundenheim, and incorporating them within its boundaries. Unlike Mannheim, Ludwigshafen does not appear to have had an overall plan, and its various sections are peculiarly unrelated one to another. It is unfortunate in being bisected by a broad ribbon of railway tracks. These include the main lines to its chief railway station (a terminus near the water-front) and goods lines connecting the industrial works and quays of the river-side with the large marshalling yards south-west of the town. Railroad connection with Mannheim and the east is made across the Rhine bridge, some distance south of the station, and this demands a second system of railway-lines disrupting the town. Neither are the manufacturing areas so fortunately sited as are those of Mannheim. Many factories penetrate into the actual town area, and industrial works succeed each other along the westward railway for 2½ kilometres, creating a central barrier to outward spread of the town in this direction. Port installations follow the quays along much of the town's river frontage, and the only recreational area, the Stadt Park,

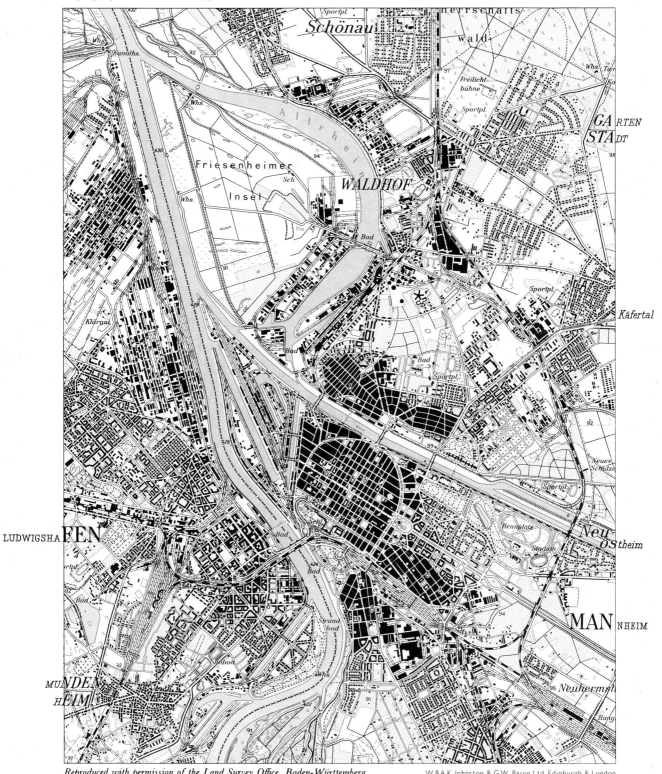

W. & A.K. Johnston & G.W. Bacon Ltd. Edinburgh & London.

which lies to the south, cannot be reached except by crossing the Luitpold Harbour. However, the chief industrial region lies to the north, and here gigantic works are immensely impressive, both in their layout and for their sheer size. The site is exceptionally favourable, with a great area of flat land for development, which has allowed unrestricted planning of buildings and railway tracks. There is nothing on the map to indicate the nature of these works, but the chemical industries of Ludwigshafen are known throughout Europe. These are the BASF works (Badische Anilin und Sodafabrik) which border the Rhine continuously for six kilometres, and cover an area of five square kilometres.

The enormous industrial development of both towns has necessitated a corresponding growth in their urban territories. Mannheim's urban boundaries extend southward to include Rheinau and Friedrichsfeld, and eastward to Seckenheim and Feudenheim. Northward it reaches the state boundary. The urban district of Ludwigshafen includes Rheingonheim and Maudach in the south, and Oggersheim, Oppau, and Edigheim in the west. In the north it includes two-thirds of the Rheinkanal, and stretches beyond it. The great spread of housing estates throughout these urban districts is strikingly illustrated on the map. Some of these are less than a kilometre apart, as in the Käfertal district, and though some are completely new creations, others are new growths around a much older nucleus (Oggersheim, Seckenheim, and many others). The exceedingly clear representation of buildings and gardens gives much information on the nature of this housing. The greatest number of houses are detached, and garden space is generous. In general, street plans are varied and open, and even where built-up blocks suggest terrace houses or blocks of flats, there are open spaces and gardens. It is obvious that these are the homes of commuters, and one is impressed by the pleasant and airy plan of these settlements—so unlike much industrial expansion of earlier days—and by the provision of many recreational facilities. A *Sportplatz* and swimming-pool are attached to even relatively small estates, and bathing in the Neckar, Rhine, and many of the lakes is provided for. As we have seen, the recreational value of the woodlands has also been recognized. All these features are less pronounced in the rural areas outside the urban boundaries. Although they are outside the state frontier and within Hesse, Lampertheim and Viernheim appear to lie within the orbit of Mannheim.

Linking these villages and small towns to the great industrial centres is a system of small-gauge railways, which circle to Heidelberg and Weinheim, connect Käfertal and Heddesheim, and extend westward beyond Ludwigshafen; while within the two cities themselves, and to all the strung-out suburbs, extends a network of street-cars. The Heidelberg-Mannheim section of the autobahn puts Mannheim into direct contact with that linking Frankfurt and Karlsruhe or the Saar, and several examples of excellently devised road junctions on these motorways occur in the mapped area.

The Growth of Mannheim

The building of Mannheim as a strong water fortress began in 1606. The fortress was built on a bluff overlooking the Rhine, and the town adjoined its walls on the north-west side, facing the marshes of the Neckar. It was itself surrounded by walls, and its streets were laid out in a grid or chessboard plan (Fig. 8). During the Thirty Years War it was attacked, and burnt down in 1622, and was completely deserted. After the war it was rebuilt according to the former ground plan, and gradually its population increased to 12,000, but it was again attacked during the War of the Palatine Succession, and razed to the ground in 1688. Refounded in 1699, it was selected as the Elector's residence in 1720, and the fortress replaced by a magnificent palace, the ramparts between fortress and town removed, and the town enlarged by the continuation of the existing streets to the palace grounds. But the court was removed to Munich in 1778, and the town greatly declined. Before it could reorient itself it suffered yet a third period of bombardments and partial destruction in the wars following the French Revolution. It became an 'open city' in 1800, and though the first part of the century was a period of many vicissitudes, in 1820 the correction of the Rhine above Altrip made the city the terminus for iron-barge river traffic. By the middle of the century commerce had enormously increased, extensive docks had been constructed, and Mannheim had become a commercial and distributing centre for south-western Germany, Switzerland, Alsace, and eastern France. When improved navigation of the Rhine brought increased competition from ports up-stream Mannheim strengthened its position by greatly developing its manufacturing activities. The increase in population necessitated an

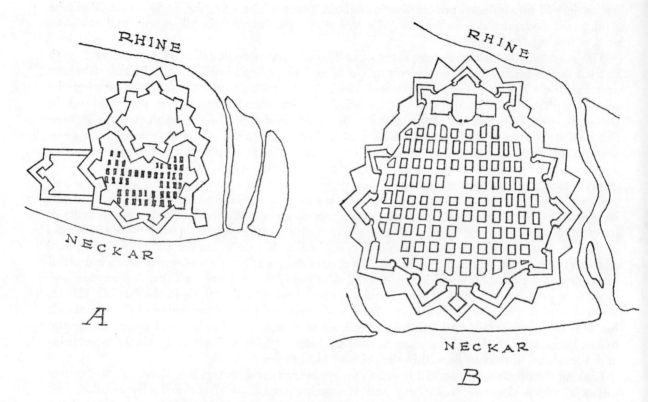

FIG. 8. STAGES IN THE GROWTH OF MANNHEIM

Based on small-scale reproductions by courtesy of the Mannheim Tourist Office

Diagram A is roughly based on an engraving of Mannheim by M. Merian (about 1620). The walled fortress overlooks the Rhine, and the adjoining walled town faces the Neckar. Together they are surrounded by a moat and outer wall. Walls are drawn as single lines, and the blocks of buildings indicate the gridiron pattern of the streets.

Diagram B is drawn on a larger scale, and is based on a map of Mannheim by J. A. Baertls in 1758. The fortress has been demolished and its place taken by the great palace of the Elector Palatine; and a new town area has been built as a continuation of the original town grid. Elaborate fortifications still surround the town.

enlargement of the town, and between 1865 and 1903 the existing streets were extended in straight lines across the green belt which had developed on the site of the former ramparts, and the moat was filled in. During this century extension of the docks and great development in the distribution of goods by rail and road has accompanied a tremendous increase in trade and manufacture, and to-day Mannheim is the leading commercial and industrial centre of the upper Rhine.

The port handles over 7½ million tons of goods annually. Vessels of 2000 tons (mainly massive barges) utilize the docks, which have an immense warehouse capacity. Many of the imports are materials in bulk—building-materials, sands and gravels, coal, petroleum, ores and minerals, timber, grain, and other foodstuffs, etc. A large proportion of these feed the great industries of the town, the oil-refineries, chemical works, steel-works, paper-works, flour-mills, etc., or are required for the building trade. Many, such as coal, timber, oil, metals, are distributed over all south-western Germany, as far as shipping and land transport will reach. The port of Rheinau is specially equipped for the handling of coal, which comes mainly up-stream from the Ruhr, with some from the Saar, to be distributed by rail. Mannheim has the second largest marshalling yards in Western Germany, and it is also linked by autobahn to Frankfurt and the north, east to Stuttgart, to Karlsruhe and the south, and west to the Saar. A host of other trades (*e.g.*, in wines and tobacco) and other industries (*e.g.*, textile, electrical) increase the variety of raw materials and finished goods handled. In 1962 the value of goods produced by Mannheim's industry reached the equivalent of £390 millions (and this did not include the building industry), and this trade and industry are very widely based.

PLATE VIII   Mannheim's Docklands (opposite p. 43)

This view looks down on the road and railway bridge linking Mannheim and Ludwigshafen across the Rhine. The web-like road junctions lying between the river and the palace of Mannheim separate the lines of traffic and prevent all intersections, and although they appear complicated they are easily manageable. The Neckar crosses the view in the background and joins the Rhine in the top left. The level of the Neckar is low, and much of its bank is exposed, but in severe floods all bridges can be put out of action. Except for the Rhinau docks, all the docklands are included, and though the Industriehafen is foreshortened in this view and hazy in the right background, with care the Altrhein can be followed to its junction with the Rhine. The map shows lock gates at the Neckar entrances to the Industriehafen, as the Neckar and Altrhein are at different levels. Since this photograph was taken (and the map published) a huge oil-refinery has been established on Friesenheimer Island, seen in the middle background. The contrast between the commercial and the industrial docks is clear. The warehouse space and railway sidings are conspicuous in the commercial docks, and barges lie along the quays, but a line of factories border the Altrhein.

For Further Study

The full map-sheet *1/50 000 L 6516 Mannheim* is essential for this study.

Stadtplan von Mannheim 1/15 000

This excellent plan, published in 1965 by the City Survey and Land Registry Office, gives all the details which the 1/50 000 map cannot supply, and illustrates the further industrial growth and urban spread of the city.

Reference

Dr Ernst Plewe, "Mannheim-Ludwigshafen—eine stadtgeographische Skizze". This is an authoritative and full account of the history and development of these cities.

(See Suggestions for Further Reading)

NORWAY

SELECTED MAP-SHEET

Topografisk kart over Norge   SHEET 1/100 000 GRADTEIG B31 AUST KYRKJEBÖ

1960

Norway has no uniform map-series of scale 1/100 000 which gives complete coverage for the whole country, but our sheet, revised in 1960, is of a type covering much of the south. It has been selected as its scale is appropriate for this massively built fjord region which has large areas almost uninhabited. The colourings used are conventional, with contours in brown; water, glaciers, and marshlands (also ferry routes) in blue; tree symbols, most cultural features, and all lettering in black. Main roads are shown in red.

The vertical interval is 30 m, but the contours are not numbered, though there are many spot heights and trigonometrical points marked. Lake surface-levels (in black) and fjord soundings (in blue) are also given, and glacier contours are shown in blue dotted lines. Tree symbols differentiate between coniferous trees (star-like symbols) and deciduous trees (circular symbols), but these are rather widely spaced, and a general picture of forest distribution is not readily obtained. Roads are well classified, and 'fair-weather' and 'all-weather' roads are distinguished. Buildings are shown in considerable detail, though a single symbol covers rather a wide range of smaller buildings.

As in all maps, the use of different styles and sizes of lettering conveys much information. Here especially the slope of the lettering distinguishes different landscape features. Rivers, lakes, and fjords are named in backward-sloping letters; mountains, spurs, and peaks, etc., are named in upright lettering; valleys, islands, headlands, and promontories in forward-sloping lettering. Settlements are also shown in italics, though district names appear in upright lettering.

Marginal information includes a scale-line in centimetres and kilometres, and a large selection of map symbols. There is no reference grid, but the co-ordinates of latitude and longitude are marked in the map-margin, with the longitude reckoned from the Oslo meridian and the relation of this to the Greenwich meridian stated. (Oslo meridian 10° 43' 22·5" east of Greenwich.)

A short selection of the conventional signs and a glossary are given below, and the names of nearly all the landscape features of the map-extract are composed in part of one or other of the words contained in this short glossary. Many names, especially of landscape features, are frequently repeated, and in the small mapped area of the Kyrkjebö sheet six summit areas are named 'Blåfjellet', and there are other examples of repetition.

The Norges Geografiske Oppmåling publishes many map-series, of scales ranging from 1/25 000 to 1/1 000 000, and these are fully listed, and index-diagrams provided, in their Kart Katalog.

GLOSSARY

dal, dalen, botn—valley. **eggje, åsen**—ridge. **elva, elvi**—river. **fjell, fjellet, bergi, berget**—mountain(s). **fjorden**—fjord. **foss**—waterfall. **haug, haugen, haugane, holten, holtane, heia, heiane, knausen**—summit(s). **hytte**—hut. **lia**—slope. **nes**—headland. **nipi, nipa, nuten**—peak(s). **nova, novi**—spur. **sæter**—mountain pasture. **stöl, stölen**—sæter hut(s). **tjörna**—small lake. **tuva**—hill. **vatn, vatnet**—lake(s).

ABBREVIATIONS

öv	. .	övre	. . .	upper		in	. .	indre	. . .	inner
ned	. .	nedre	. . .	lower		Sk	. .	skole	. . .	schoolhouse
yt	. .	ytre	. . .	outer						

SELECTED SYMBOLS

꜀꜀꜀꜀ ꞏ꜀꜀   Power transmission line, power-station, transformer station

꜖꜖꜖꜖   Aerial cableway

⊞ ✛   Church; chapel

✷   Factory, power-station

☼ ☼   Small mill; sawmill

⊙ ◇ ✳   Lighthouse; beacon; air navigation light

▪ ●   Farm; mountain pasture

▪ ▲   House, small farm, small power-station, mill, etc.

♟   Hotel, inn, tourist hut

Landscape of Fjord and Fjell: Dispersed Industrial Development

Norges Geografiske Oppmåling. Topografisk kart over Norge 1/100 000
GRADTEIG B31 AUST KYRKJEBÖ

The Sogne Fjord is the longest fjord of Norway, and cuts through a plateau of Pre-Cambrian and Cambrian gneisses at its western end, and loftier schists and crystalline highlands at its eastern end. From its mainland entrance to the head of its continuation as the Årdal Fjord, it is 100 miles long. At its head it has many long tributary branches, which penetrate deeply into some of the highest regions of the country, and snowfields and glaciers of the Jostedalsbreen and the Jotunheimen highlands lie above the tributary fjords of Fjaerlandsfjorden and Lustra-fjorden respectively. Communications by ferry and by seaplane link the fjord settlements, but overland routes leading outward from the fjord are few and difficult, and many land routes are closed in winter.

THE MAP-SHEET

Note. It is most important that the full map-sheet should be available for study, but to aid in the finding of place-names, all those that occur in the map-extract are printed in heavy type in the text.

The map represents only a very small part of the Sogne Fjord, as it requires six 1/100 000 map-sheets to give it consecutive coverage from its western sea entrance to the eastern arm, and these do not cover the main tributary fjords. The Kyrkjebö sheet, which includes **Höyanger**, is the third sheet from the west, and in spite of the limited area it covers, most of the characteristic elements of fjord landscape are represented. In comparison with its total length the fjord is of course very narrow, but nevertheless in the area shown on our map its width averages 4½ kilo-metres (about three miles). There are no submarine contours, but soundings are given in metres, and indicate the astonishing depths of the fjord trough. On the map-extract these are shown as **1295 m (over 4000 ft.) in the west, and 1233 m (over 3900 ft.) in the east**, and even greater depths (1303 m) are recorded on the full sheet. These probably mark the deepest channel of the trough, but east of **Ortnevik** three soundings are given in a line across the fjord, and the two soundings of **1215 m and 1251 m** lie 2 km apart, and so give some suggestion of the width of the trough floor. The floors of the tributary fjords are at a much higher level than that of the Sogne Fjord itself, and their submerged junctions with it must be discordant. The underwater mouths of the **Höyangsfjorden** and of the **Lånefjorden** open 829 m and 1091 m respectively above the Sogne deeps, so that these fjords are submerged hanging valleys. The number of soundings given is small, and the map cannot reveal the underwater slopes of either the main or tributary valley sides, but they will probably bear a very close relationship to the exposed slopes above the water-line. Everywhere these are steep, and particularly so in the tributary fjords, where in places they appear as spectacular towering walls sweeping up directly from the water's edge. Where fringing terraces occur along the shore, however, they provide sites for settlement, such as at **Austerheim** and its westward continuation to Kyrkjebö. Other areas of lowland are delta fans, raised beaches, and the flats at the heads of tributary fjords, and though these are often small and isolated, they nevertheless provide some of the chief settlement sites.

The main fjord walls are less dramatic, and are broken by the narrow valleys and ravines of a host of small rivers and torrents that fall from the plateau, or from sources in the bordering wall itself. But a number of larger glaciated valleys also open into this reach of the fjord. The glaciers that formed them were tongues of ice draining from a plateau surface once completely covered by an ice-cap, and so some of the features typical of a valley glacier may not occur. Corries, which are characteristic valley heads in glaciated mountains of the alpine type, are here far less numerous. The **Dalsdalen**, which continues the drowned valley of the **Höyangsfjorden**, and which has many features typical of glaciated valleys, has no corries, and gradually rises and narrows to reach the plateau. This is true also of the Indre-dalen, at the head of the Vadheims-fjorden.

To the south of the Sogne Fjord the **Stordalen** and the **Vassdalen** are short glacial troughs south of **Ortnevik**. The **Litleelva** and the **Storelva**, which drain these troughs, both have a number of head-streams. However, the valleys of these do not end blindly in their corrie-like amphitheatres, but extend beyond these far into the plateau, collecting the outflow of numerous lakes. The one exception to this is the deep hollow in which the Svartevatnet lies, with a ring of torrents falling over its walls from the plateau. A beautifully shaped and deep corrie is the Nykjevatnet farther west, receiving the waters of two tremendous torrents, one dropping over 300 m and the other nearly 200 m. The outflow of this lake, with the waters of the Brekkelva, have built a small delta at the side of the Österbövatnet. This is a lake-filled glacial basin in a continuation of the Sorbödalen, and its threshold forms a barrier between the lake and the Fuglesetfjorden and a site for the little settlement of Söreide.

The surface of the plateau shows many of the features characteristic of a region once completely covered by an ice-cap. There are no mountain peaks or 'horns', bitten by corries and shattered by frost, but a landscape worn and scoured by overall ice erosion. In the area of the map-sheet, the region south of Sognefjord has the largest areas of uninterrupted high plateau, with heights of over 800 m in the west, rising to over 1200 m in the east, and reaching 1311 m in the extreme east. This lofty surface has large flattened hummocks and innumerable shallow depressions filled with lakes of every size, and with most irregular shapes. A multitude of streams drain from the summits into the lakes, and link them together in a confused and intricate maze, but on the summits themselves there are also great numbers of small lakes, some with and some without outlet. These summit areas form water divides, but there are often no clear relief features which can be recognized as such. In many places the divide must lie between adjacent lakes, whose waters drain away in opposite directions, and yet which lie so close together that they can scarcely be shown as separate on the map. Obviously the knobs and hummocks which direct the water-flow must be extremely small. Everywhere the drainage appears disordered: some streams divide into two separate courses, some lakes have two outlets supplying streams flowing in opposite directions, river-courses are ungraded, and their pattern confused, and their waters finally fall steeply into the heads of the deep valleys which cut the edge of the plateau. Few waterfalls are named on the map, but the contours show that rapids and waterfalls must abound. (It is worth noting that in several places on the plateau lakes and linking streams string out in straight lines, suggesting lines of weakness such as might result from faulting.)

All the features mentioned are best illustrated in the southern part of the region, in the areas north of Blåfjellet in its extreme south-west, north of Sundagsfjellet in its centre, and west of Blåfjell in the eastern part. Changes in the drainage are, of course, taking place, and here in the south-east, marshy river deltas appear to be filling the Vövringvatn, and just to the north of this one of the outlets of the Budeievatnet has disappeared, to be replaced by a marshy track, as a more deeply incised outlet drains away the water of the lake.

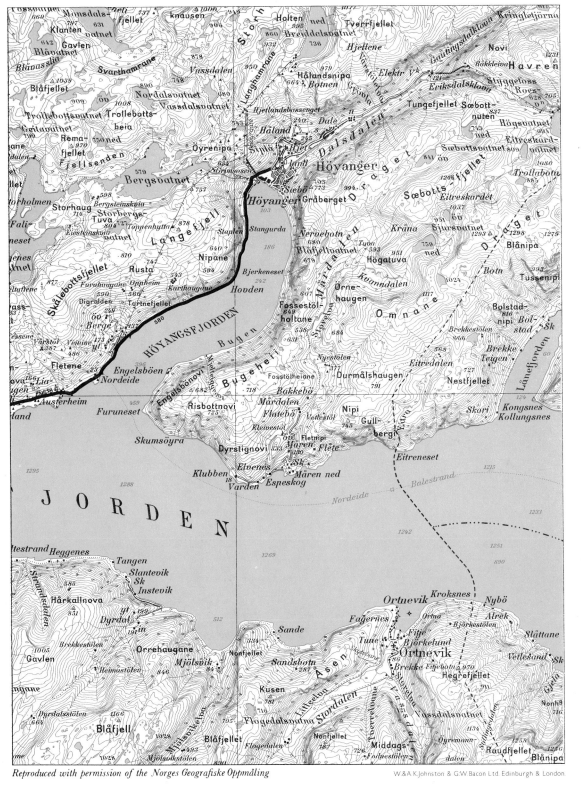

The plateau north of the Sogne Fjord has many features similar to those already described, but it differs in being far more dissected. Its rounded, lake-strewn summits rise progressively to the east, and roughly correspond in height to those south of the fjord, but they are not the highest hummocks of a continuous high-level plateau. A maze of large, deeply eroded hollows separates them into individual highland areas, which in some places have the appearance of mountains (*e.g.*, Selstadheia). As the hollows are not only deep but steep-sided, many of these highlands have very abrupt bordering slopes. **Langefjell,** south-west of Höyanger, falls steeply both to the fjord and to **Bergsvatnet**; the summits of **Remafjellet** and **Trollebottsheia**, north of the same lake, descend abruptly by the steep **Fjellsenden** to its shores, and by **Svarthamrane** to **Monsdalsvatnet**; the plateau-topped **Tverrfjellet**, north of Dalsdalen, has a drop of over 580 m to the **Gautings valley**, and of 300 m to **Breiddalsvatnet**. Most of the eroded basins contain lakes, but as only surface levels are recorded it is not possible to discover their actual depths. The high-level lakes—which are most numerous in the north—overflow into lower lakes, and the drainage consists of strings of lakes with linking streams forming an intricate pattern. The largest river is the western Storelva, which steeply descends with waterfalls (*Streksfossen*) to the Indre-dalen, and follows this southward to the Vadheimsfjorden. It is interesting to trace this river-course up-stream to its source in Holsnipa (1139 m), overlooking the Viksdalsvatnet, and to follow also its many tributary streams to their sources. Together they drain more than half of this plateau area. As the river system matures many of the lakes must disappear: some will be drained as their outlet channels are cut deeper, others will be filled in as contributory streams bring down sediment and build delta fans. That this is happening here is shown by the creation of a marshy delta at the head of **Monsdalsvatnet**, and the partial obliteration of lake Lonene, which has been half filled by two delta fans. Marshes farther down-stream may represent dwindling or drained lakes. In many other areas, also, marshy tracks and patches appear to indicate the disappearance of lakes, and the small lakes on summit areas are far less numerous than south of the fjord.

To the south-east of Dalsdalen the plateau has a somewhat different character. The highland forms are simpler and more compact, and the drainage better integrated. The south-eastern **Draget** summit (1298 m) is the only height of the mapped area with permanent snow. Four very small snowfields occur on the northern slopes, and are indicated on the map by blue dotted contours.

It is obvious from the map that most of these highlands are above the treeline. The latitude here is higher than that of the Shetlands, and much of the plateau surface lies over 900 m (about 3000 ft.), with the highest summits reaching well over 1220 m (about 4000 ft.). But forests cover the fjord walls and many of the valley sides, and though the tree-limit cannot be accurately determined, trees are shown to reach 610 m (about 2000 ft.) in many places, and occasionally 700 m on sheltered valley slopes and around some of the plateau lakes. Most of the trees are seen to be deciduous. At low levels these may be of various north European species, but at high levels they are almost certain to be stunted birch-trees. Coniferous forests are shown in the north-west and extreme north-east of the area represented on the full sheet, and eight sawmills are marked. Five others are shown near hamlets or larger settlements on the southern shores of the Sogne Fjord, and they probably supply local needs. All but two of the mills are situated on mountain torrents or on the shores of strongly flowing rivers, suggesting the use of water-power.

Apart from forest, marshland is the only vegetation cover mapped. As we have seen, this occurs in widespread patches at many levels, even on the summits. The cold heights can have no parallel in British moorlands, and must approach nearer to the vegetation of the tundra, but though they are not specifically marked, it is clear that mountain pastures cover large areas at lower levels, and especially near the numerous lakes. Here there are *saeters*, the Norwegian counterpart of the Swiss *alp*. Sheep and young cattle graze on these in the summer months, and still in some areas, dairy herds. The buildings, or *stölen*, so numerous on the map, are the temporary homes of those who tend or milk the animals. Clearly marked paths, often steep and long, link these lonely huts with the coastal and valley settlements. A scattering of fishers' and hunters' cabins suggest that there is still much wild life in these relatively unpeopled highlands, and game may well augment the meagre resources of the more isolated hamlets and solitary farms.

But the limited forests and more extensive pastures are not the chief resources of the plateau. The high-level water-supplies in the numberless lakes, and the streams that drop to the deep valleys with tremendous force, have provided exceptional opportunities for the development of hydro-electric power. The **Bergsvatnet,** west of Höyanger, is drained by an unnamed stream which drops down the plateau edge to the flats at the head of the Höyangsfjorden, and the waters of **ned Breiddalsvatnet** also fall steeply into the **Dalsdalen** before reaching Höyanger. It is obvious that the water-supplies of these two lakes have been utilized for the development of power. The map does not give much detail, and it is not possible to detect whether dams have been built to increase the storage capacity of these lake-reservoirs, which are naturally great. The Bergsvatnet is very extensive, and the Breiddalsvatnet, lying in a glacial basin, is probably of great depth. Both lakes are fed by copious mountain streams and by overflow from higher lakes. Höyanger can therefore tap great water reserves, with heads of 579 m (1899 ft.) and 736 m (2474 ft.) respectively. Cableways lead from stations at the lake outlets to a centre (probably the main power-station) adjoining the industrial works on the water-front. Only one power transmission line is mapped, and this crosses the **Langefjell** to **Berge.** Another large power-station is shown some distance up Dalsdalen, at the foot of the **Eriksdalsklova,** with its violent fall of waters from the eastern plateau. The lake reservoirs utilized here are the **Högsvatnet,** 694 m, and a still higher lake mapped on the adjoining sheet, the Nordalsvatnet, 804 m, which is fed by snowfields. At both power-stations a lift or rack-railway links the plateau and the valley. It is clear that Höyanger utilizes a great supply of power, and that the potential supplies are so abundant that further development is possible. This asset, and the economy of easy sea transport, will have favoured the growth of industry—especially the smelting of aluminium ore, which requires very great supplies of power. The map does not state the nature of the industrial works shown, but they are in fact those of the Norsk Aluminium Company. Other associated industries will certainly have developed, and the town has become a small industrial centre—an alien settlement in a once remote and austerely beautiful region.

The Western Fjords and Industrial Development

There are now many isolated industrial centres in the western fjords, and at the head of the Sogne Fjord itself Årdal has bigger aluminium works than Höyanger. The supreme advantage of these sites is their cheap and abundant water-power. The rainfall is heavy, and the glacial lakes of the plateau provide high-level heads of water and great opportunities for water-storage. This is particularly important as winter snow causes a serious reduction of water-flow during many months. The modern practice is to build underground power-stations and to cut tunnels through the solid rock for the water-intake, and the hard, tough rocks of the region lend themselves to this tunnelling. Often it is possible to dig tunnels in the floor of an over-deepened glacial lake, increasing its storage capacity to the whole content of the lake basin from surface level to bottom outlet.

Although the sites are far from the coast, transport of raw materials and manufactured goods is cheap. The fjords—except in tributary branches far inland—do not freeze, and sea transport adds little to the cost. Moreover, sites for large industrial plants (that would be difficult to find in any built-over area) are available at many fjord heads. As a result of all these factors, many electro-chemical and electro-metallurgical industries have grown up in situations similar to Höyanger.

Though fjord sites have many economic advantages, for the industrial communities there are problems. The towns are isolated, and their small size imposes many limitations. The geographical setting is beautiful, but the winter is long, the rainfall is heavy, and all too often the mountains are smothered in cloud. The impact of the tourist industry, and of the industrial developments, on the small farming communities of these regions has been great. The way of life followed by generations is changing. Many of the more inaccessible *saeters* are abandoned, and milk lorries climb daily in summer to those that remain in use. The cattle are fed in the valleys on rotation grass, and some cash crops are cultivated, including fruit—in Höyanger, pears and plums.

The Norsk Aluminium Company

This company was founded in 1915 to produce aluminium by means of electric power from the Höyanger Falls. Its works have been repeatedly modernized, new power-stations built, and its power capacity increased. Bauxite is imported from the Company's mines in southern France, and the smelting works provide the alumina for the production of metal, which in 1965 reached

PLATE IX.   Höyanger

28,000 metric tons. Most of the aluminium is transported to Holmestrand, near Oslo, where finished aluminium goods and rolling-mill products are manufactured.

PLATE IX Höyanger (opposite p. 56)

The town of Höyanger lies at the head of its tributary fjord, at the entrance to a narrow corridor enclosed within massive mountain walls. These rise almost sheer on the right (south-east) to Gråberget, 2550 ft., and on the left only slightly less steeply to 2600 ft. above Dale. The valley is U-shaped in section, and the absence of interlocking spurs gives it an open aspect, so that the view extends uninterruptedly for over 3¼ miles. Forests, apparently deciduous, cover the lower slopes, but in many places the steeper walls are composed of exposed rock, and the rounded summits are treeless. In the background to the left the foreshortened ridge of Skinger-fjellet stands out clearly, culminating in the summit of Skardfjell, which is just beyond the region of the map-extract. In the far distance two other rounded summits appear, one of which seems to be patched with snow. On the right, in the middle distance, the slopes and spurs of Havren close the view. The straightened course of the Dals river can be recognized just behind the town, and its outlet to the fjord in the left foreground, while far in the background a light streak probably indicates the fall of the tributary Gauting into the Gautingsdalklova.

The town itself and its all-important industrial works (the Norsk Aluminium Company) borders the waters of the fjord, which, quiet and deep, allow the direct import of the raw materials—bauxite from France. Over the town hangs a haze of smoke, which the still air—indicated by the unruffled surface of the fjord—cannot disperse. The smoke inevitably disfigures the landscape, and most probably pollutes the air to some extent. The photograph shows the whole valley bathed in sunlight, but this is a cloudy and rainy land, and one wonders how often the mountain walls disappear into a low blanket of mist, and for how long on the rarer sunny days they shut out the sunlight and warmth and throw a chill shadow over the town.

Maps for Further Study
Northern Europe (Norway) 1/250 000 Sheets NP 31, 32–10 *Målöy*
Series M515 Edition 2-AMS NP 31, 32–11 *Årdal*

The M515 series is one of the official Norwegian map-series, and these two sheets give a complete coverage of the Sogne Fjord and most of its branches, and include the ice-covered area of the Jostedalsbreen and the mountain heights of the Jotun Fyell.

The maps have been prepared by the Army Map Service, United States Army, and they have been compiled from the topographic maps and hydrographic charts of the Norges Geografiske Oppmåling, and printed by them. In this edition (2-AMS) an English translation of all marginal information is given, and a glossary is printed on each sheet.

PLATE X. The Coen Harbour, North Sea Canal (opposite) *Photo K.L.M. Aerocarto*

THE NETHERLANDS

SELECTED MAP-SHEET

Topografische Kaart van het Koninkrijk der Nederlanden 1/50 000 25 WEST   AMSTERDAM
1961

This Netherlands map-sheet is one of a complete and up-to-date series which covers the whole country. (However, as will be noted later, since some years elapse between map revisions, no map can record all the latest changes, especially in a country where great developments are in progress.)

The landscape shown is very representative of the country, as it covers large areas of polder, both meadow and croplands, and also includes a number of important urban centres. There are no hilly heathlands, and only in the extreme bottom right-hand corner of the map-sheet are any contours shown. On the other hand, part of the coastal sandhills are mapped. Though heights above or below sea-level are supremely important in this land reclaimed from the sea, the representation of relief (shown by contours at 5 m intervals) is not a dominant feature of this map-face, and details of land-utilization make a far greater impact.

The landscape is man-made, and man's control is everywhere apparent. The small ditched fields are shown in detail, as are all the installations by which they are preserved and the waters around them held in check. This demands large numbers of finely drawn symbols, and differentiation is made between steam, motor, and electrical pumping stations, windmills, small windmills, water-mills, and wind-motors. Similarly, not only are there symbols for beacons, lights, and tidal limits, but arrows are drawn to indicate direction of water-flow and of tidal changes of flow. Even the position of tide gauges is given. All these signs, and many others, are drawn in black, as are the multitude of ditches outlining the fields. Also in black are marsh and tree symbols, orchards and tree nurseries, embankments and dykes (classified), glasshouses, and all buildings (apart from completely built-up urban blocks), railways, and all lettering.

Nevertheless, this is the most colourful map studied. Overprints of dark green, pale green, buff, and yellow distinguish areas of forest, meadow, heath, and sand respectively. Arable land is uncoloured. Also, much use is made of red colouring. Pale red is used for completely built-up urban areas, and though within these the roads are left white, all other metalled roads are coloured either brilliant red or orange. Suburban roads are shown in orange, and also country roads less than 6 m in width. Finally, a bright blue is employed for all inland waters, and a paler blue for marine waters.

Marginal information is detailed, and a very full list of conventional signs is provided. All information is in Dutch, French, and English. Longitude is measured in degrees from Greenwich, and the Dutch datum (NAP—the mean sea-level gauged at Amsterdam) is related to those of Germany and Belgium.

Topografische Dienst, Delft, publish an excellent catalogue of all their map series. This is illustrated by complete map-indexes and six map-extracts.

GLOSSARY
hoogspanningsleiding—high-tension line. **hoeve**—farm. **meer**—lake. **vaart**—canal. **ven**—fen.

ABBREVIATIONS

Basc br	. Basculebrug	. bascule-bridge	Oph br	. Ophaalbrug	.	. drawbridge
Dr br	. Draaibrug .	. swing-bridge	PK	. . Protestantsekerk	.	Protestant church
Fabr	. Fabrieken .	. factory	Pl	. . Paal	. .	. pole
Gdr	. Grondduiker	. earth culvert	Sch sl	. Schutsluis	. .	lock
Km	. Korenmolen	. corn-mill	Sl	. . Sluis	. .	. sluice
		Wt	. Watertoren	.	. water-tower	

SELECTED SYMBOLS

●   Church tower, tower, high dome

○   Church without tower

✫   Lighthouse

◉   Church tower, tower, high dome ⎫
                                ⎬ Known co-ordinates

✪   Lighthouse ⎭

    a meadows—field boundaries on pale green background
    b orchards
    c tree nursery   *d* glasshouses   *e* arable land
    f deciduous forest—tree symbols on dark green background
    g needle-leaved forest—tree symbols on dark green background
    (Heath land shown in buff on the map, and sand in yellow)

    a windmill   *b* watermill

    a small windmill   *b* wind-motor

                 a steam
Pumping-engines: *b* motor
                 c electric

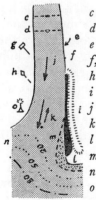

    c   ferry
    d   ferry for pedestrians
    e   tide-gauge
    f, g kilometre posts on river banks
    h   beacon
    i   dike with reinforced slope covering
    j   arrow showing direction of flow
    k   indication of tides
    l   high-water mark
    m   low-water mark
    n   depth-curves
    o   beacon (light)

    (The stipple represents blue colouring on the map)

The Netherlands are one of the most densely peopled countries of the world, with an average of over 900 persons per square mile. But the country is small, parts are under water, and parts are infertile, and most of the good agricultural lands have been won from the sea only by the skill and effort of her people. Nevertheless, the country is not only able to produce foodstuffs for her domestic market and for the manufacture of various food products, but has become one of the world's chief exporters of a number of these—eggs, potatoes, potato flour, condensed milk, and cheese. Her resources in raw materials are meagre, yet her industries have so greatly expanded that they engage over 40 per cent of her working population, and they range from heavy industries to those of the greatest delicacy. However, though not naturally richly endowed with either good agricultural lands or with industrial raw materials, the country has had great opportunities for commerce, so that for centuries she has maintained commercial relations with the Baltic countries, through the Rhine valley with the heart of Europe, and overseas with all the countries of the world.

North Holland is one of the eleven provinces of the Netherlands, the second in density of population, and one of the most vigorously developed. The region covered by the map-sheet lies in this province, and the features which it illustrates are related to the facts that have been briefly outlined above.

THE MAP-SHEET

The colours used in this map-sheet have given it a striking pattern, distinguishing clearly three types of landscape—sandhills, polders, and industrial urban areas.

The western sandhills border the North Sea, but only a tiny stretch of the coast is included in the extreme north-west of the mapped area. (The dunes formerly continued unbroken across the present entrance to the North Sea Canal, which has been cut through them.) They are irregularly heaped and vary greatly in height, and with individual dunes reaching over 120 ft. they provide a protective barrier. Their wooded eastern slopes form a welcome contrast to the completely level lands at their feet, and it is obvious that they are valued for recreation, and as highly favoured residential sites.

By far the largest area of the mapped region is polder, and everywhere the small fields bounded by ditches, the network of canals, the miles of protecting embankments, and the ubiquitous pumping-station bear witness to the labour, care, and vigilance of the Netherlands Government and the Dutch farmer. For these farmlands are not drained peatlands as in our Fen country, but croplands and meadows created from lakes, or won from under the sea, and all maintained far below sea-level. The mapping of arable lands without colour and of meadowlands in green distinguishes in the mapped area four main polder regions—two arable and two meadowland. An irregular arc around Haarlem, and a spread of country west and east of Zaandam, are the two areas of polder meadows. Haarlem and its polders are bordered on the west by the sandhills and (until the middle of the last century) were bounded on the east by the Haarlemmer Meer (Lake), and protecting dykes make a clear demarcation between the older polderland and the reclaimed lake. The fields around Haarlem are small, and irregular in shape, size, and pattern, and they probably represent successive eastward reclamations through many centuries. To the south, suburbs have encroached upon the polders, and the fields are particularly small, with many narrow cultivated strips and patches of woodland among the pastures. Such small strips are certainly very intensively cultivated, and a few orchards and glasshouses suggest that some may be market gardens. The growth of Haarlem has also covered some of the eastern polders, and at the present time new housing developments are being carried to the limit of the eastern municipal boundary.

The second area of polder meadows is part of a far larger region, and stretches from the Zuiderpolder (109497) and Assendelft in the west to Oostzaan in the east, and far beyond the mapped area to the former Zuider Zee (now the Ijssel Lake). All these polders are enclosed by a high protecting dyke, with sluice gates and locks to provide escape of drained waters and permit

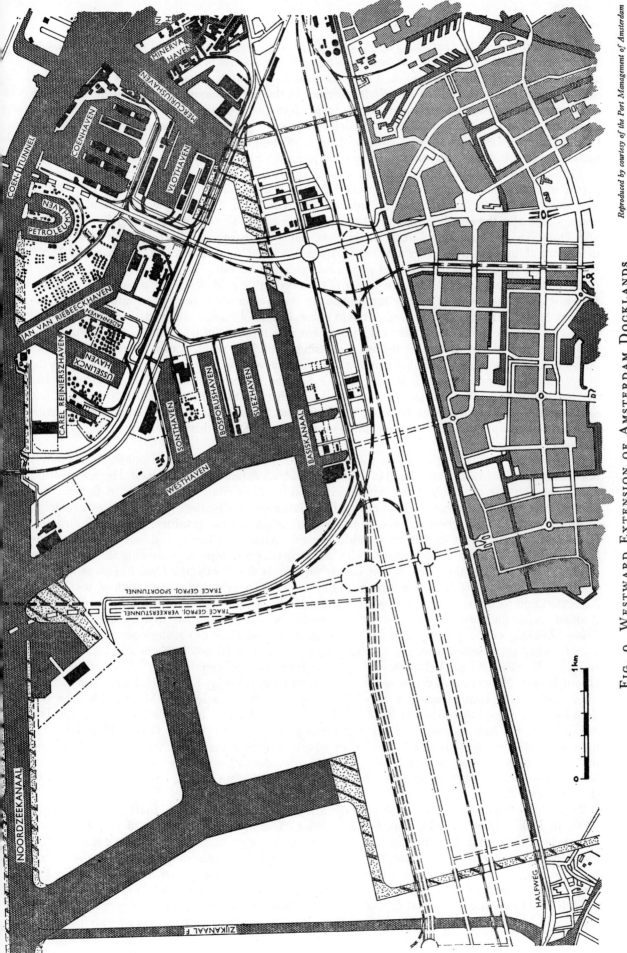

FIG. 9. WESTWARD EXTENSION OF AMSTERDAM DOCKLANDS

KEY: Black areas represent sheds, warehouses, and industrial works.
Dark stipple represents water areas. Light stipple represents urban buildings.

traffic in and out of the canals. The Assendelft polder closely resembles that of the Haarlem district, except that the land appears more waterlogged, and scores of small wind-pumps are shown, as well as larger pumping stations. The Veenpolder, separately enclosed, seems to have been drained more recently, and the De Wyde Wormer in the north-east also appears to be a modern reclamation of extremely waterlogged lands. The Zaan river, bordered by the industrial town of Zaandam, flows through a polder area which has in some places almost as much water as land. In these there is no network of roads, and no footbridges cross the water-channels. The map shows eleven windmills, but these are probably preserved for their great interest and beauty, and it is unlikely that they provide power for any industrial activity, or that they are used to any extent in drainage. Bascule-, swing-, and draw-bridges provide crossings over the river Zaan, and locks and sluices control the junctions of the river with the broad water-channels of the polders, and also the entry of the river into the Zijkanaal G. The towns of Assendelft, Westzaan, and Oostzaan are strikingly linear settlements, each consisting of a narrow line of buildings strung out along both sides of a single road. Assendelft stretches nearly four miles from the North Sea Canal to the limit of the mapped area, and probably beyond.

The Haarlemmer Meer Polder, the larger of the two arable polder areas, is a complete contrast. It is obviously the result of a very large-scale drainage operation, the reclaiming of the Haarlemmer Meer (in 1853). The rectangular grid of canals and of roads, with each section subdivided by ditches into rigidly rectangular fields, the linear development of farm-houses along the roads, and settlements placed at two right-angled crossings, build up an obviously planned and wholly man-made landscape. The heights given on the map show that much of the area lies 14–15 ft., or even more, below sea-level. It is completely ringed by dykes, and electric and motor pumping stations abound. Apart from the runways and buildings of the Amsterdam Airport and a few areas such as that around Nieuwe-Brug, the farmlands are cultivated, and the number of farms shown on the map indicates that their lands must be limited, and this cultivation certainly highly intensive.

Just outside the enclosing dyke, on the south-east side, a very specialized polder area extends north-east from Aalsmeer at the head of a large lake which extends far south-west. Here, as around Zaandam, the narrow polders are separated by wide water-channels, and are in fact narrow islands. The area specializes in orchards and in glasshouse cultivation. Oosteinde, rather drier, is almost covered with glasshouses, and the output of glasshouse products must be enormous. It is certain that Amsterdam must provide a great market for these, and one wonders if the factories within the area are concerned with some forms of preserving or processing these products.

The second great arable area is that which surrounds the North Sea Canal. This is also the result of a large-scale reclamation scheme. (The IJ was formerly a westward arm of the Zuider Zee extending to the sandhills, and when the North Sea Canal was built the IJ was completely drained except for the canal channel.) The boundaries of the reclaimed area are the old coastal dykes (Zeedijk) of the polder lands already described, and their old water-courses and canals, once opening into the sea arm, are now carried across the reclaimed lands as Zijkanaals. These comprise Zijkanaal A near Velsen-Noord, and the clearly marked canals B and C from Spaarndam, D and E from Nanerva and the Westzaner Overtoom respectively, F from Halfweg, and G from the former mouth of the Zaan. Many of the features of the Haarlemmer Meer Polder are also found in this area, but part of it has probably already changed its character (Fig. 10). (The expansion of the Amsterdam docklands has made great inroads upon the Groote IJpolder. This map was published in 1961 (after revision in 1958), and since then enormous progress has been made in the completion of Westhaven, and new dry docks have been excavated west of this dock basin. Ultimately another great harbour west of Westhaven will carry the docklands to the Zijkanaal F.)

The urban areas covered by this map-sheet are of exceptional interest. Haarlem is the capital of North Holland, and an old, once fortified, town. The northern boundary of the old town is the obvious zigzag canal bordering the former bastions (now turned into public gardens). On the west the canal narrows and continues southward; and then turns eastward to join the Buiten Spaarne, which formed the eastern boundary of the town. We have seen that some residential areas are sited in the sandhills and spread along their eastern margins. But Haarlem is not just a residential town and provincial capital. It is seen to be a canal port, with wharves and a small dock basin, and the many factories marked show it to be—to some extent, at least—an industrial

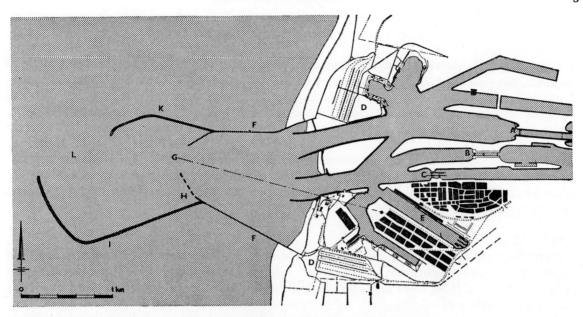

FIG. 10. NEW HARBOUR ENTRANCE AT IJMUIDEN

Reproduced by courtesy of the Port Management of Amsterdam

A. Northern Lock (1930).
B. Middle Lock (1896).
C. Southern Lock (1867).
D. Storage yard.
E. Construction and transhipment harbour.
F. Existing piers.
G. Existing harbour entrance (width 850 ft., draught 35 ft.).
H. Demolished pier.
I. New southern pier under construction.
K. New northern pier under construction.
L. New harbour entrance (width 2300 ft., draught 50 ft.).

town. Spaarndam, with its ancient windmill, its wharves, quays, small dock basin, and locks, is also within its municipal territory.

The map shows that Zaandam is an important port and manufacturing town. Its long wharves front the Zaan river and parts of the Zijkanaal and North Sea Canal. The dock basin of Hembrug is within its territory, and a new developing dock basin on the eastern side of the Zijkanaal. A number of factories and industrial buildings are shown along its crowded river-front, and also along those of its neighbours farther upstream. (But there is much that the map cannot record, for Zaandam has a long industrial history. Here was invented the wind-driven sawmill, and for long the town stood first amongst the industrial centres of the Netherlands, with a forest of windmills—flour-mills, oil-mills, sawmills. To-day it has a wide range of manufactures and tremendous barge traffic on its river.)

Only the western outskirts of Amsterdam are mapped on this sheet, but they show clearly the city's widespread advance over the countryside. As Haarlem makes smaller advances over the polders eastward, Amsterdam makes giant strides westward. Several big and carefully planned garden suburbs are shown (though unfortunately not named), and other areas left uncoloured on the map represented in 1958 new extensions in process of building—but these will now be completed. Much of this new housing appears to consist of large blocks, possibly of flats, with apparently communal garden space. Smaller terraced housing can also be distinguished, but the small detached house and garden for a single family appears very rare. Public gardens and recreation grounds are generous in size and well laid out, and in the Amsterdamsche Bosch a very fine park is provided, with woodlands and open spaces and facilities for sport. Amsterdam's western expansion represents extreme care in planning. Polder lands cannot be converted into building-sites without long, costly, and elaborate preparation, and new suburbs must combine attractiveness of design and provision of amenities with economy of space.

Enormous westward expansion has also been undertaken in the docklands. The map does not include the great waterfronts of the city, north and south of the IJ, with their multitude of harbours, but younger dock basins excavated on the south side of the North Sea Canal are shown. These include harbours bordered with warehouses and some factories, and provided with rail and road services, and a basin set apart for the discharge and storage of petroleum. Still newer harbours lie farther west, which at the time of the map revision were unfinished, but where a number of industries had already been established. The map shows clearly that the North Sea Canal area provides outstanding opportunities for development, not only for commerce but also for industry. It adjoins the most highly industrialized region of the Netherlands, and has abundant space for the excavation of deep-water docks, for open or covered storage, and water frontages for factory buildings.

THE MAP-EXTRACT

Apart from sandhills and polders (already discussed), the four main features of this small but important area are the entrance locks to the North Sea Canal, the town of IJmuiden, the great industrial works of Hoogovens and other smaller works, and the Velsen railway and motorway tunnel under the canal.

The map shows the inner part of the North Sea Harbour entrance, and the four sets of locks that separate the sea from the canal. The largest lock is the Noordersluis, and the Middensluis and the Zuidersluis—the last with two lock basins—give entry to progressively smaller vessels. The size of the Noordersluis and the width of the canal make it clear that it is designed for use by the largest cargo vessels. Its depth is not given, but it has recently been increased to a water-depth of 50 ft. Along it great liners and the largest modern tankers, general cargo-carriers, and great bulk carriers can pass each other in safety and reach the docklands of Amsterdam and berth at her quays. It will be noticed that the colouring of the canal is that of the rivers, and not of the open sea, and the canal is actually filled with waters of the Rhine, and is a man-made mouth of the Rhine, though its link with this river (the Amsterdam-Rhine Canal) does not appear on our map-sheet. The lock gates of the Noordersluis, that keep out the sea, are gigantic in size and strength, and when closed they link the roads shown on the map and provide a bridge for motor and pedestrian traffic.

IJmuiden came into being after the canal was opened (in 1876) and, as is seen by its two sea harbours, the Visschershaven (fishery harbour) and Haringhaven (herring harbour), it has become an extremely important fishing-port and fish-distributing centre. (Its harbours open into the North Sea inner harbour entrance, and are protected from silting by the great piers of the extensive outer harbour entrance, beyond the map.) Its wharves are well served by double-track railways, and two double tracks serve the long buildings on the wharf of the Visschershaven. These are obviously fish-markets or auction halls. IJmuiden is in fact the greatest fishing-port of the Netherlands, but its chief importance lies in the industrial development on the opposite side of the canal.

Hoogovens is the name given to the Royal Netherlands Blast Furnaces and Steelworks. As the plan of the works suggests, the blast-furnaces occupy the southern half of the site, and the steel-works lie to the north. (Both have since been greatly extended.) The map shows that ocean vessels can unload raw materials from overseas at the tidal Hoogovenshaven without entering the canal, and that there is ample space for berthing, and for the temporary storage of materials in bulk. Similarly, dock basins opening from the canal penetrate into the works-site, and link it with the Rhine and other inland waterways. Therefore, although these works are far from coal, ore, or limestone supplies, all these can be imported easily and cheaply and without transhipment, and the finished products as easily and cheaply distributed. Light railway tracks and roads form a network over the site, and link it with the main railway and motorway systems.

The Velsen Tunnel provides for a double-track railway and a motorway under the canal. As is clear from the map, the single excavation has provided separate tunnels for rail and road; and also (though this is not apparent) completely separate carriage-ways for the motorway. The tunnel is straight, and the union of both rail and road has obviously necessitated some diversion of the railways, and the very careful junctions of the tunnel roads and the main surface roads are

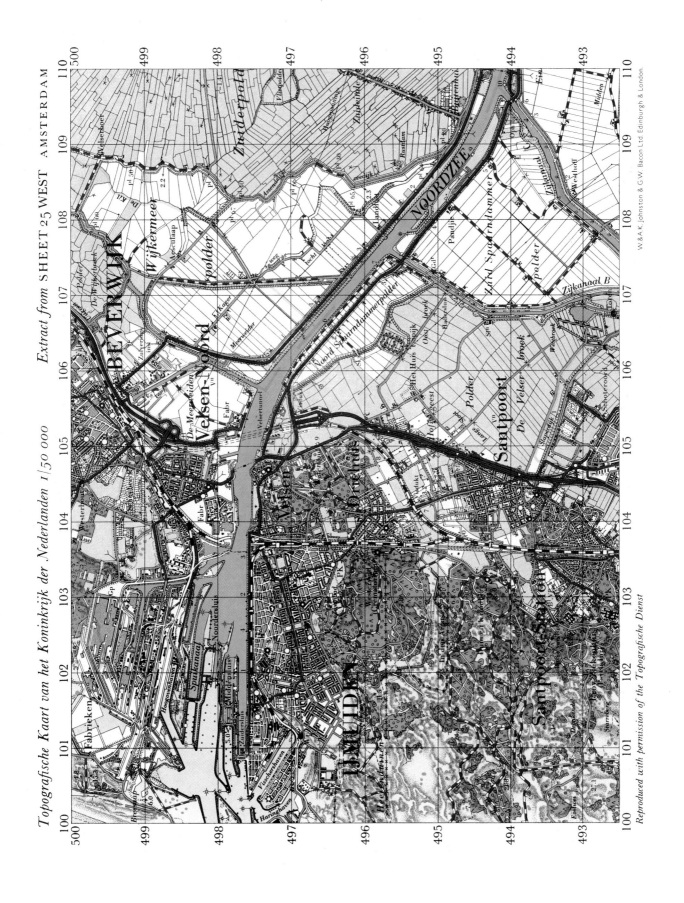

Topografische Kaart van het Koninkrijk der Nederlanden 1/50 000

Extract from SHEET 25 WEST AMSTERDAM

W.& A.K. Johnston & G.W. Bacon Ltd Edinburgh & London.

Reproduced with permission of the Topografische Dienst

BEVERWIJK

Wijkermeer polder

Zuiderpolder

NOORDZEE

Velsen-Noord

Zuid Spaarndammer polder

Santpoort

De Velser broek

Polder

Santpoort-Zuid

IJMUIDEN

Spaarnkanaal

Noordersluis

Middensluis

Zuidersluis

Velsertunnel

Zijkanaal B

conspicuous on the map. The old ferry—seen west of the tunnel—is now superseded (except for slow traffic, and for motor vehicles carrying such goods as chemicals and explosives).

FIG. 9 *Westward Extension of Amsterdam Docklands* (p. 61)

It is clear from this map, which shows the progress already made in the dockland extensions, that three great enlargements are completed. Westhaven has been increased to double the size shown on our map-sheet, as a number of new basins and subsidiary basins have been added. To the west of the Westhaven entrance a new graving dock has been built, which will accommodate vessels of 100,000 tons. Still farther west a second immense harbour, already over two miles in length, will in the near future surpass the Westhaven in size, and bring the docklands halfway along the North Sea Canal. Even this does not complete the extension plans, which include another, larger dock basin in a huge westward expansion. As can be seen, the canal itself is being widened, and at the same time deepened to a water-depth of 50 ft., so that all the enormous docklands of Amsterdam will be open to the largest ocean vessels. However, these developments do not only provide for an increase in commerce; around Westhaven and westward there are hundreds of acres available for industry, and many sites have already been utilized. Amsterdam is not only increasing her ocean-borne traffic. In 1952 the Amsterdam-Rhine Canal was opened, and since then her trade with the Rhine ports and industrial areas (always important) has vastly increased. In the eight years between 1952 and 1960 it increased sevenfold. It is obvious that Amsterdam is one of the greatest links between Rhine and ocean shipping, and that she will have an immense transit trade. Modern installations at her docks have perfected the handling of cargoes, so that they are loaded and unloaded with the utmost care and dispatch, and her warehousing facilities are equally well developed.

FIG. 10 *New Harbour Entrance at IJmuiden* (p. 63)

This diagram shows in thick black lines the new entrance of the harbour. To accommodate vessels of increased tonnage the harbour is being deepened by the removal of obstructions—sand-bars and war-time wrecks—to give a clear waterway of approximately 48 ft. There is no need to widen or deepen the Noordersluis: its dimensions at the time of its building were such that it is able to accommodate the largest vessels. The enlargement of the harbour entrance is being accomplished by the extension of the existing piers, the south pier to about two miles and the north pier to one and a half miles. The asymmetrical harbour pattern prevents silting, as tidal currents are caused which scour the entrance. During the building of this harbour—an outstanding engineering feat—the Visschershaven has been used as a construction harbour, and great storage yards have been built for the materials required. These materials included two million tons of stone blocks, each weighing over a ton, and one and a half million tons of gravel.

PLATE X The Coen Harbour, North Sea Canal (opposite p. 57)

The photograph shows the Coen Harbour from the north. It is for the exclusive use of foreign flag-carriers, and the piers from the right are the America, Africa, Asia, and Europe piers respectively. The loading and unloading equipment and the warehouse facilities are obvious. South of this basin, in the Vlothaven, is the enormous grain terminal of the International Grain Transhipment Company. The nearer of a double row of twenty-four grain elevators is clearly seen, and two grain-carriers are being unloaded simultaneously by mobile pneumatic suckers, discharging the grain into the elevators for storage, or directly into holds of giant barges. The elevators have a storage capacity of 50,000 tons, and together the suckers can discharge grain at the rate of 1600 tons per hour. To the right of the elevators a long general-cargo pier is in course of construction, and over the top of the elevators a timber warehouse is seen, with a discharging vessel. This lies on the Mercurius Harbour, into which the Vlot Harbour opens, and it has a depth of 50 ft. The North Sea Canal and the entrance to the Coen Harbour are right in the foreground of the view, and to the left, at the entrance to the Mercurius Harbour, is a large superphosphate works—the Albatros Fertilizers Plant.

It is interesting to note the changes that have taken place in the Vlot Harbour since the publication of the map.

For Further Study

Topografische Kaart der Nederlanden 1/50 000 25 OOST AMSTERDAM

This sheet, which adjoins that of the map-extract, includes many features of great importance. Together the two sheets give a complete coverage of the North Sea Canal, and of the city of Amsterdam and its huge docklands. The urban plan of Amsterdam is clearly shown, and is of exceptional interest (see R. E. Dickinson, *The West European City*). Also of interest is the pattern of fortifications surrounding the old towns of Weesp and of Naarden in the south-east of the mapped area.

A short length of the Amsterdam-Rhine Canal and its entrance into the North Sea Canal lie also within the mapped area, and this barge canal has enabled ocean and inland shipping to meet, enormously increasing the trade of Amsterdam.

A wealth of valuable information has been published by the Port of Amsterdam Authority, and a fine folder-map *Amsterdam—Gateway to the Common Market*, and a very well-illustrated booklet *Amsterdam—Sea and Rhineport* have been published by the Amsterdam Port Association, N.Z., KOLK 28, Amsterdam C.

UNITED STATES OF AMERICA

SELECTED MAP-SHEETS

Department of the Interior. Geological Survey
SHEETS *1/62 500*   MICHIGAN   JACKSON QUADRANGLE *1935*
PENNSYLVANIA   PITTSBURGH QUADRANGLE *1904*

These two map-sheets are selected primarily on account of the landscapes they cover. The Jackson sheet is very finely drawn, with contours at 10 ft. intervals, minute symbols very clearly shown, and light and open lettering. It is typical of a great number of revised 1/62 500 sheets, where some changes—notably the inclusion of colour overprints (forest green, etc.)—have modified the appearance of the original map. The sheet is a 1964 reprint. The Pittsburgh sheet is out of date, and was reprinted without further revision in 1957. It has been chosen to show the location of industrial works at the beginning of the century. It is fortunate for the studies which follow that both sheets retain the details of town plans and buildings, although in the latest maps of the Geological Survey built-up areas of over three-quarters of a square mile are mapped as "building omission areas", and are coloured in an all-over light red, with only 'landmark' buildings and main roads distinguished.

It is important to place these sheets within the broad plan of the National Topographic Map Series of the U.S.A. Both maps belong to the same series—*i.e.*, the 15-minute Series—and they cover a quadrangle of 15 minutes of latitude and 15 minutes of longitude, and are mapped on the scale 1/62 500. The Jackson sheet extends from lat. 42° N. to 42° 15′, and from long. 84° 15′ W. to 84° 30′ west of Greenwich. A larger-scale series is the 7½-minute Series, mapped on the scale of 1/24 000. Both these series are produced by the Geological Survey. A smaller-scale map is the U.S. 1/250 000 of quadrangle size 1° (lat.) × 2° (long.), and this series, prepared by the Army Map Service (AMS) and published by the Geological Survey, almost completely covers the whole country. Large areas are not yet covered by the 7½′ and 15′ quadrangle maps, and a continuous programme of fresh surveys and revision of existing maps is carried on year by year. Most of this is mapped on the scale of 1/24 000.

Map-indexes for each state are published by the Geological Survey, showing sheet lines and names, with dates of revision. The Michigan index of 1964 contained 551 published maps of the scales 1/24 000 and 1/62 500, but still there were some areas of the state not mapped on either scale, and the index showed many maps older than that of Jackson. There is no later edition of the Jackson map. The Pennsylvania index contained 773 published maps of the 7½′ and 15′ series. The Pittsburgh area is covered by much more up-to-date maps on the 1/24 000 scale, as well as the special map "Pittsburgh and Vicinity" mentioned in the text.

The Geological Survey also publishes an informative booklet in colour "Topographic Maps", which includes, among much else, the full list of symbols and small illustrative map-extracts of the three scales mentioned above.

SELECTED SYMBOLS

   Depression contours (in brown)

School

Glacial Drift Landscape: Michigan

U.S. Department of the Interior. Geological Survey 1/62 500 MICHIGAN
SHEET JACKSON QUADRANGLE

The mapped area lies west of Detroit, in the southern part of the great Michigan peninsula between Lakes Huron and Erie on the east and Lake Michigan on the west. It is a region once covered by the ice-sheets of the Quaternary Ice Age, and its surface features are due to glacial deposition. The area represented in the whole map-sheet is covered with glacial drift. In the northern part this is composed of a ground moraine of boulder clay and of fluvio-glacial gravels deposited when the ice was retreating. In the southern part of the area there is a hilly region of terminal moraine (the Kalamazoo Moraine). These hills form a low watershed in the extreme south of the state, and two of its main rivers, the Grand River and the Kalamazoo River, rise here and flow eastward to Lake Michigan.

The smaller towns of southern Michigan are involved in the great industrial activities of Detroit, which is the fifth largest industrial area in the U.S.A. The enormous motor-vehicle industry of this city requires for its assembly plants a vast variety of component parts, and this has resulted in a widespread development in the manufacture of these parts, not only in the metropolitan area but in a ring of towns outside the city and throughout the whole of southern Michigan. Jackson, which is partly within the mapped area, is only 64 miles west of Detroit, and is most probably concerned in some of these industries. The town lies on a main road between Detroit and Chicago, and on a direct rail route linking these two cities.

THE MAP-SHEET

The region represented in the map-sheet is one of low relief, composed of a disorderly distribution of small irregular hills and hummocks, separated by shallow depressions and pitted by countless hollows. In this confusion of small relief features there are more continuous channels, some of which contain permanent streams and others intermittent streams, and which are nearly all marsh-filled. Lakes occur everywhere, and are of all sizes and shapes. An endless repetition of these features builds a monotonous landscape typical of glacial drift.

The terminal moraine, composed of more pronounced hills, occupies much of the districts of Liberty, Somerset, and Woodstock, with large areas over 1100 ft., and many hummocks reaching considerably higher levels. There is no clearly defined boundary between these and the ground moraine of the north, where there are lower and more irregular mounds to the west of the Blue Ridge, and a drift or till plain to the east.

In an area where boulder clay and outwash sands and gravels have been unevenly distributed there are certain to be numerous hollows and lakes, but here a large proportion of the hollows are 'kettle holes' and the lakes 'kettle lakes'. Isolated masses of stagnant ice were wholly or partly buried by drift deposits when the ice-front was in retreat, and when the ice masses melted the drift cover or surround collapsed, forming enclosed basins of very irregular shapes and sizes. Two examples of kettle lakes are Mud Lake in Liberty and Perch Lake in Somerset, but there are numbers of other kettle holes, ponds, and lakes—great and small.

Two other features present in glacial drift are 'kames' and 'eskers'. Kames are mounds of ice-contact stratified drift, and some are formed of sediments which accumulated in crevasses or in surface hollows in stagnant ice, to be deposited when the ice melted. Other kames may take the form of small deltas which were built outward from a stationary ice-front by emerging englacial streams. When the ice melted the deltas were left with steep slopes where the sediments had been banked against the ice, and a fan of gentler slopes spreading forward. Kames are not easily recognized in the map in the profusion of irregular hummocks and hollows, but there is a probable kame delta to the south of Skiff Lake, where a roughly fan-shaped series of mounds, with steeper slopes to the north, reaches 1120 ft.

Though kames are difficult to identify with certainty, the esker included in the extract area is so striking that it cannot be mistaken. (See the Map-extract section below.)

The drainage of the area is poorly integrated, and the few main streams are immature. A

68

United States Department of the Interior. Geological Survey 1/62 500

Extract from SHEET MICHIGAN. JACKSON QUADRANGLE

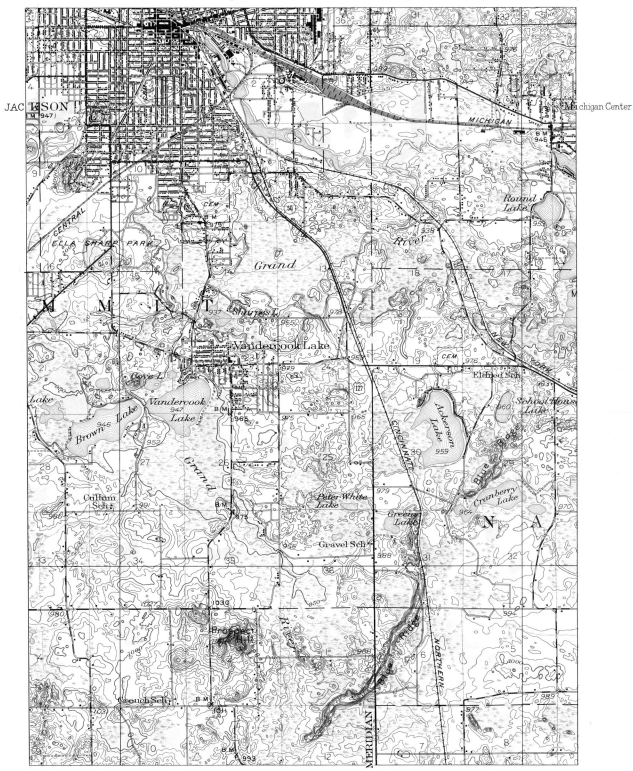

W.&A.K. Johnston & G.W. Bacon Ltd. Edinburgh & London.

string of linked lakes gives rise to the Grand River, and its early course consists of two stretches of sluggish meanders through channels filled with marsh and woodland, separated by a swifter reach in a narrow valley cut in the low hills. Its course shows several complete changes of direction, until it finds a gap in the Blue Ridge, and turns again to wander northward. Marshy channels abound, and in the north-west many are probably abandoned glacial channels. In the south-west also there is a maze of shallow valleys with a confused drainage pattern.

Apart from Jackson and its suburbs, this is a thinly peopled area with very few settlements. Many lakes are so surrounded by marsh that they offer no possible building-sites, but where their shores are drier they may be almost completely enclosed in a fringe of settlement. This occurs around Clark Lake and parts of Round Lake and Lake Ackerson. A few other lakes have some development in depth with small road-networks. However, excluding the lake shores, there are only four settlements in the mapped area which are large enough to have any road-network, and these are all sited near the junction of road and railway. Other, smaller communities consist of a cluster of houses, and perhaps a school or church at a cross-roads. But if settlements are few there is a considerable dispersed population, and everywhere homesteads are strung out along the roads. Schools are often solitary, or accompanied only by one or two other buildings, and they must draw their pupils from considerable distances.

The area is covered by a close, mainly rectangular road-grid, and there is hardly a building shown at any distance from it. This is a most distinctive road pattern, probably laid out by the original surveyors, but the routes of the state roads and national roads (both numbered on the map) have been planned without reference to the grid.

THE MAP-EXTRACT

The surface features of hummocks, hollows, and lakes have already been discussed, and part of the landscape of the area will be studied later in relation to the aerial photograph. The most striking physical feature, however, and the one for which the extract was chosen, is the beautifully formed esker, the Blue Ridge. Only part of it is included, but its characteristics are excellently shown. It is a discontinuous six-mile ridge, with a sinuous course. It rises to 1050 ft., and is narrow and steep-sided, crossing indiscriminately an irregular floor ranging from 950 ft. to 980 ft. The map gives no indication of the materials of which the ridge is composed, so that it is by shape alone that it can be recognized as the deposits of a subglacial or an englacial stream. The deposits carried by the stream, in its channel below or within the ice, were either left as a ridge when the ice melted or they were spread out into a fan where it issued from the ice-front, and were continued as a ridge which grew backward as the front of the ice retreated.

Two other features of special interest are the confused and in places artificial drainage of the Grand River valley below Vandercook Lake, and the urban pattern of Jackson.

Vandercook Lake receives the waters of the meandering Grand River, but an intermittent stream also links this river with Brown Lake. The natural outlet of the latter follows a circuitous course to the wide marshes south of Jackson, falling six feet in about three miles. But Vandercook Lake has an obviously artificial outlet northward, which drops ten feet in one mile to Sharpes Lake. Ultimately its waters, with those of Brown Lake, flow in a straight man-made course through the marsh, and the meanders are cut out, the flow regulated, and the speed increased. Farther down-stream the widened river would appear to have been dammed to form narrow basins above the town.

Although only the southern part of Jackson is included within the map area, it provides an excellent example of the 'gridiron' town plan so typical of the American interior. It is particularly clearly mapped, with minutely drawn symbols for individual buildings, and with all schools as well as churches marked. Only two straight roads cut obliquely across the rigidly rectangular pattern of well-spaced built-up blocks composing the main body of the town. However, it covers an area of small hills, so that the roads must vary in slope, and there is a little less rigidity in the road patterns covering some hillocks in the suburbs of the west and south.

The main part of the compact town centre is shown to lie on the western side of the Grand River Valley, followed also by the railway which bisects the town. (It is quite possible that the railway is as old, if not older, than the town.) Jackson is now an important railway junction, and the southern section of its web of lines is clearly shown and named on the full map-sheet. Its large marshalling yards and many of its track junctions lie to the south-east, about a mile up the valley from the town centre. The river here is widened into a series of long, narrow lakes, and considerable industrial development has taken place along their borders, with large buildings served by single or multiple railway tracks. Other such industrial buildings are shown on the town's eastern fringe. There is obviously no centrally placed hub for radiating road routes, and main long-distance through roads join a trunk route enclosing the southern town on its outskirts, while only one main traffic route crosses the town centre from east to west.

Large marshy areas and channels prevent an even outward spread of the town, and suburbs have developed around the higher margins of neighbouring lakes and on raised hillocks. Vandercook Lake and Michigan Center are two such suburban growths, both grid-planned. The former appears to be wholly residential, but Michigan Center has some industrial activity. In Vandercook Lake and Ella Sharp Park expansion has been provided for by the completion of the road plan of new suburban districts in expectation of their build-up.

PLATE XI Glaciated Country south of Jackson

The district covered by this vertical photograph lies wholly within the mapped area. The northern lake shown is Lake Ackerson, with School House Lake to its east, Cranberry Lake to its south, and the lakes Peter White and Greens easily identified farther west. The Cincinnati Northern Railway crosses the region from north to south, appearing on the photograph as a thin white line west of Ackerson Lake, and the old U.S. route 127 (coinciding with the Michigan Meridian) crosses the area in the same direction as the railway, and is also shown as a white line. This now swings westward and away from the old route 127 at the cross-roads north of Peter White Lake (elevation 979), and then turns northward parallel to the old 'light-duty' road. All the other roads of the map can be recognized on the photograph with ease, as can each of the woodlands and marshy tracts.

Features of relief are not so readily identified, and the esker, which is excellently illustrated on the map, cannot be picked out immediately on the photograph. However, in the south-west between the motorway and the railway, it can be recognized by the woodland which outlines its shape for a short distance, and then by a small summit footpath which joins the light-duty road crossing the summit obliquely. Here the pale colour of the eastern slopes, illuminated by the morning sun, is contrasted with the darker grey of the western slopes, and helps to define its shape. The northern extension of the esker, with the parallel railway on its eastern side, can be traced as far as Peter White Lake, and then less easily around the western end and to the north of Cranberry Lake. In several places irregular white patches at the base of the esker ridge can be recognized as quarries or pits, probably gravel pits. These occur to the east of the ridge in the south, and to the west of the ridge opposite Greens Lake. There seem also to be some pits or excavations immediately south of the western end of Cranberry Lake.

The lakes appear to be deep, but Lake Ackerson, of which the floor has two basins, has two areas of shallow water. Cranberry Lake has a marshy margin at its western end, which is crossed by the long paths leading from its residential fringe to boat-houses at the water's edge, and which provides an inferior site to that of the houses around Lake Ackerson. Two small lakes marked on the map appear to have dwindled or dried up. One is marked south of Lake Ackerson at the edge of the Blue Ridge and the other in the marshes west of the same lake. Some shallow oval patches of marsh, east and west of the southern esker, give the appearance of having been originally lake-filled.

But the photograph is valuable more for its record of the land-utilization of the region than for its coverage of glacial features. It is obvious that agriculture has been pushed to the limit of cultivable land in a region with relatively large areas of water and marsh. In the wetter areas grasslands (appearing dark grey) extend to the borders of the marsh trees and bushes, but on slightly higher ground rectangular fields are usual. Much paler colouring probably denotes tilled fields, and these are less numerous. The orderly rows of trees around some buildings are orchards.

There is no settlement nucleus shown in the photograph, but houses line the eastern margins of the two largest lakes, and other buildings are strung out at irregular intervals along the roads. This is the settlement pattern of the whole region as shown by the map. The lakesides are attractive residential sites, and boat-houses line the water-edge. Farmhouses are not in the midst of their

PLATE XI.   Glaciated country south of Jackson

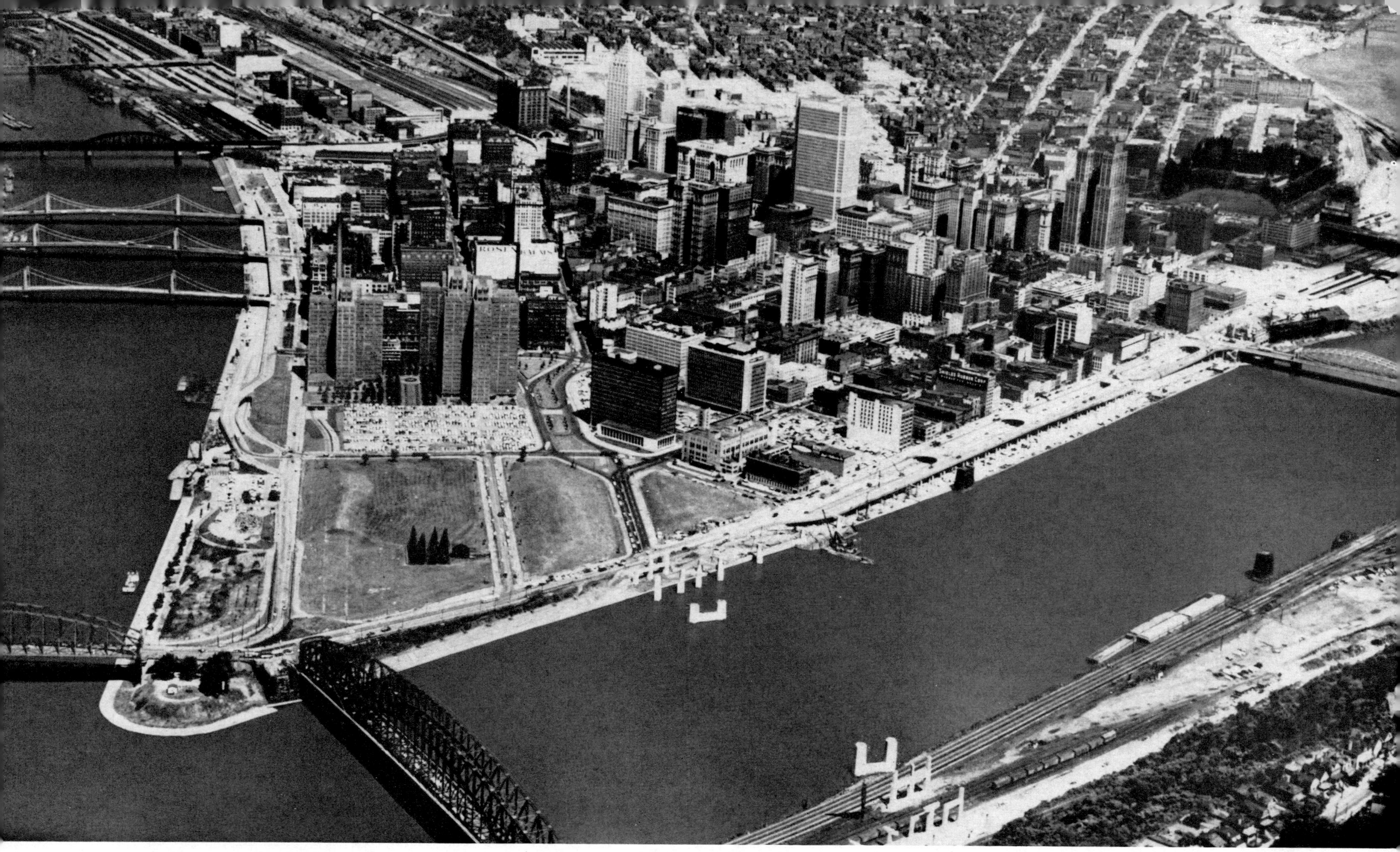

Photo: Paul Popper, Ltd.

PLATE XII. Pittsburgh, at the junction of the Allegheny and Monongahela Rivers

fields, but on the roadside, and the number of houses along the road in the north-east corner of the photograph area suggests that this also is being developed as a residential area.

The whole district lies little more than three miles from Jackson, and yet its 7½ sq. miles is still rural in character, with no industrial intrusion, nor the disfiguration which is so often found on the fringe of an urban centre. It is interesting to note how few changes had taken place in the twenty-nine years which elapsed between the mapping of the area (1935) and the aerial survey which produced the photograph (1964). With the exception of the new motorway, the routes of roads and railways remained the same, buildings did not increase in great numbers, and the western end of Cranberry Lake and the road-sides in the extreme north-east were the only new residential areas. Woodlands and marshlands remained substantially the same, but, as we have seen, two small lakes have partially or completely disappeared.

For Further Study

For a most valuable map, which includes the lobate border of the great northern ice-sheet at the time of the deposition of the Kalamazoo moraine, see Fig. 90, page 202, W. W. Atwood, *The Physiographic Provinces of North America*. Figs. 74 and 88 are also most relevant.

Pittsburgh Region: Industrial Concentration and Continuance

U.S. Department of the Interior. Geological Survey 1/62 500 PENNSYLVANIA
SHEET PITTSBURGH QUADRANGLE

The industrial district of Pittsburgh has its centre in the great city covering the triangle of land between the converging Allegheny and Monongahela rivers, which unite to form the Ohio. These rivers cut deeply into the Allegheny Plateau, which falls gently from the abrupt scarp of the Allegheny Front and its parallel ridges in the east, to the central plains in the west. The plateau is composed of horizontal layers of Palaeozoic rocks, including many limestones, sandstones, and clays. Interbedded with these, and at various horizons, are the coal-seams of the extensive Appalachian Coalfield. Here many of the coal-seams occur at a sufficient height to underlie the plateau summits and outcrop on the valley sides.

THE MAP-EXTRACT

This extract is part of the 1/62 500 map-sheet 'Pittsburgh', which with the adjoining sheet 'West Pittsburgh' covers the city and the industrial areas developed around its river-fronts. The sheets are the latest 1/62 500 maps of this district published by the Geological Survey. New map-sheets of scale 1/24 000 were produced in 1948 and 1953, and in 1960 a special map-sheet of 'Pittsburgh and its vicinity' was published on this same scale. Fig. 11 is a sketch map of exactly the same area as that of the map-extract, and it shows selected features from this 1960 map, but reduced to the scale of 1/62 500. The two maps together—the second more than half a century later than the first—give an exceptional opportunity of illustrating the great urban spread, and the concentration and continuance of heavy industry, in spite of technical changes and the explosive growth of new competitive areas.

The area shown lies six miles south-east of Pittsburgh, and is part of the dissected Allegheny Plateau, where flat-topped summit areas reach over 1200 ft. A multitude of small streams cut into the plateau, and fall steeply to the river Monongahela, its tributary the Youghiogheny, and the much smaller Turtle Creek. The larger rivers swing in big loops within their deeply incised valleys, but these are so narrow that the strips of valley floor are no more than a quarter of a mile wide, and often much less, and the valley sides above the outer curves of the loops rise in places to over 400 ft.

The map shows clearly that at the beginning of the century industrial works were established wherever there were available sites on the valley floor, and that such sites were very limited in extent. Although it gives no direct information as to the nature of these works, one can reasonably assume that it shows the forerunners of the smelting and metal industries of to-day. It is likely that the Bessemer works were blast-furnaces, and that Rankin, Duquesne, and McKeesport, each with a similar industrial layout, also had smelting-works. Provision for the tremendous traffic in heavy and bulky raw materials and finished products is seen in the ribbons of multiple track railroads. Necessarily these used the valley routes, following the base of the plateau walls on both sides of the rivers. But though the river valleys were immensely important highways, for both rail and water transport (the full sheet shows three river locks and many jetties), their depth and narrowness imposed great limitations. The industrial sites were too cramped, giving little space for future expansion, and the railroads had to follow sinuous river-courses, and were sometimes even cut into the valley walls.

Adjoining the works and climbing the valley slopes, the map shows closely built industrial housing. In many instances the gridiron patterns of streets were not coherent parts of a town plan, but were merely agglomerations of houses, discordant with the relief, as in northern Duquesne and eastern McKeesport, or covering steep slopes in ladder-like terraces, as in eastern Rankin. This ill-planned urban spread surrounding the industrial works indicates the extremely rapid growth of the labour force at the beginning of this century.

However, this small map gives little indication of the geographical factors which helped to bring about this extraordinary development of heavy industry, in a region which would appear to offer great difficulties. No mines of either coal or iron ore are marked. But mining would seem to be a feasible explanation of the short lengths of light railway or wagon tracks, which as the map shows penetrated into the plateau and ended blindly in its upper slopes, where only a single line of buildings, or a small group, or often no buildings at all, were marked. These were possibly mining centres or single pit-heads. South of Homestead, railway tracks (possibly mineral lines) linked these with the industrial works on the valley floor. At Camden (in the south-west of the mapped area) they were linked with the river-side, presumably by cable or suspension railway, as they were carried over the plateau edge. Similar lines are shown at Dravosburg, to the north of Camden, and at East McKeesport, though in the latter they were linked with the railways in the valley below. The full map-sheet shows a multitude of these tracks, and they definitely suggest an extractive industry in the plateau which was of prime importance to the works in the valleys, and which was possibly the mining of Appalachian coals to supply the smelting works (Coal Valley is marked south of Camden beyond the map boundary).

Many of the valley railways mapped were long-distance lines, and on the full sheets (Pittsburgh and West Pittsburgh) some of these are named—the 'Baltimore and Ohio' (marked as B and O on the extract), the 'Pittsburgh, Cincinnati, Chicago and St. Louis', and the 'Pittsburgh and Lake Erie'. It is not possible in the extract to distinguish these last lines from others within the broad bands of railways shown, and their enormous importance, in carrying to the Pittsburgh smelting-works the high-grade iron ore from the Lake Erie ports, is not revealed. These ores came from the shores of Lake Superior, and all through the summer were shipped to the ports of Lake Erie. Endless streams of ore-filled trucks then piled up stocks at the smelting-works to last through the winter, when the supplies would be cut off. It is obvious that the huge ore dumps reduced still further the limited space of the narrow industrial sites, and that great numbers of railway sidings were required.

Fig. 11 is a sketch-map of the extract region, showing a few selected features from the large-scale 1960 map. More than half a century has brought about many changes, but there are also remarkable similarities. The most noticeable change is the growth of built-up areas. The towns have spread over the plateau to meet each other, and so form a small part of the great Pittsburgh conurbation. On the other hand, some earlier housing areas, shown in the older map-extract, have been cleared to make room for the extension of industrial works. This has taken place in the north-west of Homestead, on the water-fronts of Port Perry, Duquesne, and a smaller area of McKeesport. There has been much improvement in industrial housing since the turn of the century, and doubtless the new housing areas will be more attractive and far less closely built than the old.

Although many of the industrial works are considerably enlarged, and some have gained ground-space at the expense of old housing, along the water-fronts they remain in almost exactly the same positions as at the beginning of the century. But the handicap of their cramped sites is very noticeable, particularly in the Bessemer and East Pittsburgh works, where great economy of space was required in development and growth, even awkward positioning of buildings in the former. Completely new works have been built at Camden, requiring the levelling of a con-

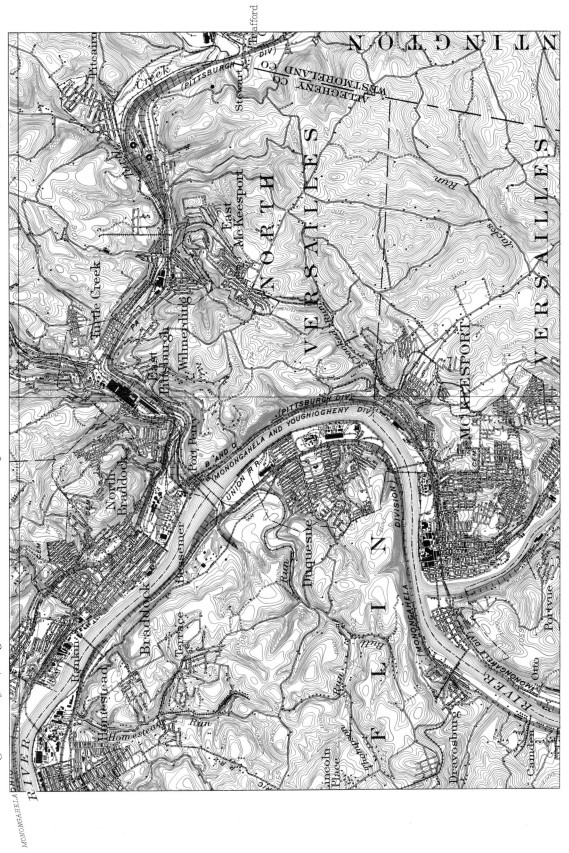

United States Department of the Interior.
Geological Survey 1/62 500

Extract from SHEET PENNSYLVANIA. PITTSBURGH QUADRANGLE

W & A K Johnston & G W Bacon Ltd Edinburgh & London.

siderable area of ground to provide the necessary site, and either new works or great enlargements have taken place at Port Vue, on both sides of the river Youghiogheny, and at Wilmerding and at Trafford on Turtle and Brush Creek respectively.

It is clear that these heavy industries do not move easily from their long-established positions in the valleys and on the river-side. The value of the river for transport and for water used in industrial processes, the multitude of railroads that of necessity keep to the valleys, the enormous capital invested in the buildings and installations of the works, and the industrial labour supply immediately at hand are all factors that tend to tie them to their present positions.

There is no indication of any mining in the small mapped area west of the Monongahela, now very largely built over, but one wonders if the golf-clubs and cemeteries (so widely shown in the 1/24 000 map) cover some of the former mining areas. However, 'strip mines' are shown in a number of places east of the river, and the mined rocks appear to outcrop on or around the summits at between 1100 and 1200 feet. The outcrops coincide closely with the contours and the rock layers must therefore be almost horizontal.

The few slag dumps mapped are a reminder that smelting and mining produce great quantities of unsightly waste materials, and the mines and their dumps, the broad tracks of ore and coal-carrying trucks, and the huge works themselves in their smoky valleys have made this district the Black Country of North America.

The Pittsburgh District

The city of Pittsburgh is at the heart of one of the greatest industrial regions of the United States, and first among the steel-producing regions. The steel industry was developed here in the first place chiefly because of the occurrence close at hand of excellent coking coals and both iron ores and limestone in the Allegheny Plateau. The horizontal coal-seams were easily mined, and though the deeply dissected plateau was not well suited to heavy industry, its rivers provided valuable routeways. Pittsburgh itself lies at the junction of the two Ohio head-streams, the Allegheny and the Monongahela, and industry has spread along these valleys in miles of great smelting- and steel-works. The local iron ores were soon surpassed by the higher-grade ores from west of Lake Superior, which were shipped to the ports of Lake Erie. Easy rail routes to these ports were provided by the valleys of head-streams and tributaries of the Ohio, such as the Allegheny with its tributary French Creek, and the Beaver with its tributary the Mahoney, which reach to within a few miles of the Lake Erie shores. However, it was not the natural resources alone that accounted for the extraordinary development of steel-production, but also the vigour and enterprise of early industrialists, chief amongst whom was Andrew Carnegie, who first introduced into the region the Bessemer process in smelting. Today great changes have taken place in smelting processes, and coking coals are not required in such quantity. Changes have also taken place in the sources of the supplies of iron ore; much of the best of the Superior ore has been extracted, and ores from Labrador and scrap metal are taking its place. At Gary, near Chicago, and in many ports on the shores of Lake Erie other steel-works are challenging the Pittsburgh supremacy. They are of great size and most modern construction, their raw materials are as easily assembled, and they have ample room for expansion. But the resources of the Pittsburgh region are immense. Though the chief mining areas have shifted westward, the Appalachian coalfield underlies a vast area, and petroleum and natural gas are also abundant, with innumerable oil- and gas-wells. Besides these the plateau has fine sand, and also supplies of clay; and glassware and clay products are exceedingly important. In fact the region is the chief centre for their production in the United States. The huge size of the Pittsburgh conurbation, the many large towns of varied manufactures within a small radius, the net of routeways, the coal-mines, the oil and gas wells, all indicate the intense industrial activity of the region.

For Further Study
Eastern United States 1/250 000 Sheets NK 17-11 CANTON
 NK 17-12 PITTSBURGH

In this series Pittsburgh is bisected by the map boundaries, and the two map-sheets named above are required to give it complete coverage. The sheets were prepared by the Army Map Service and published by the Geological Survey in 1962 and 1964 respectively, and they cover an area extending across the Allegheny Plateau from the 'fold zone' beyond the Allegheny Front in the east to the beginning of the Central Plains in the west. They therefore include the whole Pittsburgh conurbation and many of the big industrial towns along the Ohio and its tributaries. The careful mapping of coal-mines, oil-wells, and gas-wells is of very great value, and though built-up town areas are coloured yellow, and only landmark buildings and through roads are marked, the map is the most useful for a general study. The 1/24 000 map mentioned in the text is inconveniently large for a general study of the whole district, the sheet measuring 50″ × 69″.

It is assumed that the full map-sheet 1/62 500 'Pittsburgh' will be available for study, as it shows clearly the concentration of industry in the valley floors, and this does not appear in the maps mentioned above.

KEY TO FIG. II (*opposite*)

1. The closely built-over urban districts are shown in oblique-line shading. Outside these districts there is much building but of a more open character.
2. Industrial works are shown in solid black. Size, shape, and site of each individual building is approximate.
3. All the railway tracks shown are multiple, except a few short, linking lines in the sidings south of Pitcairn. Narrow bands of railway track are shown by single lines, but where there are broad ribbons of track the approximate boundaries of these are drawn. Small lines serving individual industrial works are omitted.

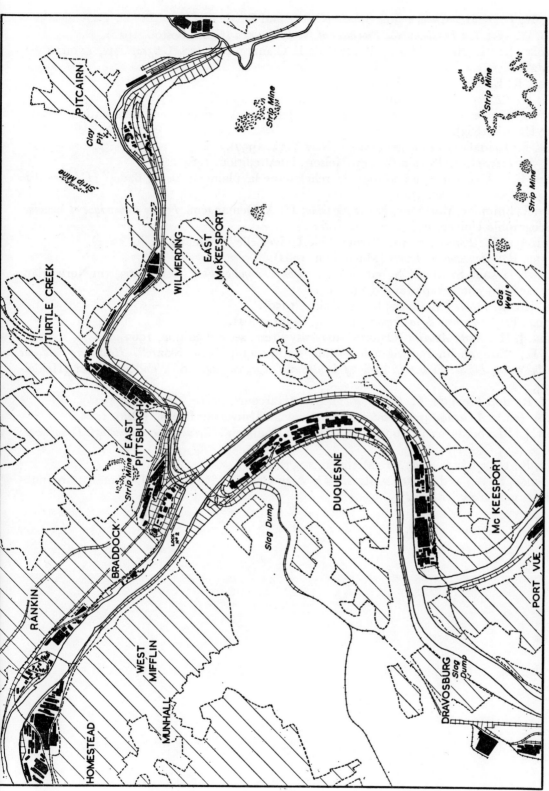

Fig. 11. Sketch-map to show the 1960 Distribution of Industrial Sites and of Urban Spread within the Map-extract Area

(Key opposite)

Based on the 1/24 000 map-sheet 'Pittsburgh and its vicinity'. Geological Survey. U.S. Department of the Interior

ARKELL, W. J.: *Jurassic Geology of the World* (Oliver and Boyd, 1956).

ATWOOD, W. W.: *The Physiographic Provinces of North America* (Ginn, Boston, 1940).

BETHEMONT, J.: "Le riz et la mise en valeur de la Camargue" (*Revue Géographique*, Lyon; 1962, No. 2).

DICKINSON, R. E.: *Germany* (Methuen, 1953).

—— *The West European City* (Routledge and Kegan Paul, 1951).

Digest of the Kingdom of the Netherlands—Economy (Netherlands Government Information Service, The Hague, 1963).

FLINT, R. F.: *Glacial and Pleistocene Geology* (New York, 1957).

HOLMES, A.: *Principles of Physical Geology* (Nelson; latest edition, 1964).

JUILLARD, E.: "Une carte des formes de relief dans la plaine d'Alsace-Bade" (*L'Information Géographique;* 1949, No. 3).

La France: I. Emm. de Martonne, *France physique;* II. A. Demangeon, *France économique et humaine.* "Géographie Universelle" (Armand Colin).

DE MARTONNE, E.: *Europe Centrale.* "Géographie Universelle" (Armand Colin, 1931).

MILLWARD, R.: *Scandinavian Lands* (Macmillan, 1964).

MYKLEBOST, H., and STROMME, S. (ed.): *Norge, Book 1. Land og Folk* (Oslo, 1963) (in Norwegian, but excellent photographs and diagrams).

ORMSBY, HILDA: *France* (Methuen; latest edition, 1950).

PINCHEMEL, P.: *Géographie de la France* (Armand Colin, 1964).

PATERSON, J. H.: *North America* (Oxford University Press; second edition, 1962).

PLEWE, E.: "Mannheim–Ludwigshafen—eine stadtgeographische Skizze". *Heidelberg und die Rhein-Neckar Lande: Festschrift zum 34 Deutschen Geographentag.* Ed. Wendelin Klaer (Heidelberg, 1964).

SMITH, J. R., and PHILLIPS, M. O.: *North America* (Harcourt, Brace, New York, 1940).

SOMME, A. (ed.): *A Geography of Norden.* "Scandinavian University Books" (Oslo, 1960).

VONFELT, J.: "La bordure vosgienne entre Sélestat et Rouffach" (*Revue de Géomorphologie Dynamique;* Paris, 1955, No. 1).

WALKER, F.: *Geography from the Air* (Methuen, 1953).

WOOLDRIDGE, S. W., and MORGAN, R. S.: *The Physical Basis of Geography* (Longmans; first published 1937, many editions).